WITNESSING AND SURVIVING
THE HOLOCAUST

WITNESSING AND SURVIVING
THE HOLOCAUST

EMERICH ROTH

Translated by
FARAH DAVARI

Copyright © 2022, Emerich Roth

All rights reserved. Printed in the U.S.A.

No part of this publication may be reproduced or transmitted in any form or by any means, electronic or mechanical, including photocopy, recording or any information storage and retrieval system now known or to be invented, without permission in writing from the publisher, except by a reviewer who wishes to quote brief passages in connection with a review written for inclusion in a magazine, newspaper or broadcast.

Quantity Purchases:

Companies, professional groups, clubs, and other organizations may qualify for special terms when ordering quantities of this title. For information, email info@ebooks2go.net, or call (847) 598-1150 ext. 4141.
www.ebooks2go.net

Published in the United States by eBooks2go, Inc.
1827 Walden Office Square, Suite 260, Schaumburg, IL 60173

ISBN: 978-1-5457-5495-5

Library of Congress Cataloging in Publication

To my dear sister Elisabeth, who gave meaning to
my life when all hope was lost.

To my dear son, Thomas, who like many other
survivors' children has endured so much pain.

To all the positive students and teachers
who have inspired me to write this book.

CONTENTS

1. My Crime: I Was a Jew 1
2. The Idyll of My Childhood.......................... 7
3. The Rise of Anti-Semitism 15
4. News of Horror................................... 21
5. Our Home in the Ghetto........................... 27
6. Resistance Meant Suicide 32
7. My Name Became a Number 36
8. Why This Cruelty?................................ 40
9. Setback for the Germans........................... 46
10. A Death March for My Father 51
11. Liberated by the Russians 58
12. I Was a Skeleton with Live Eyes 64
13. Back Home 70
14. My Journey Begins............................... 77
15. To Italy and Back Again 86
16. Finding Love..................................... 91
17. From the End to a New Beginning 99

CHAPTER 1

MY CRIME: I WAS A JEW

You have probably heard this story, or one similar to mine, once before. It is the story of one of the most horrid crimes in the history of humankind. The one referred to as the Final Solution to the Jewish Question, or *Nacht und Nebel*, in German, meaning "night and mist." Which is, of course, paraphrased in more or less poetic words instead of using the accurate term, *Holocaust*, or the annihilation of an entire ethnic group. In other words, cruel and cold-blooded murder.

Emerich is my name. I am an old man now, shaped by the experiences of a rich and diverse life. Although a rich life doesn't always mean a safe and happy one. This book is about the story of my life during the Second World War and about what took place inside the German concentration camps. Surely, you have seen countless images from those extermination camps—blurred photographs showing mass graves, where piles of corpses had been neatly stacked as wood, or rows of corpses hanging in gallows. All against a grotesque background of watchtowers and electrified barbed-wire fences. Images that, despite their context, are illusively displayed. Images of an inapprehensible malice, difficult, not to say impossible, to grasp. Perhaps you have also watched documentaries that show people standing in long lines, heading toward gas chambers and execution. You can sense horror, total impotence, and deepest humiliation, sometimes even a desperate kind of hope, regardless of the fact these flickering footages were often captured by clumsy amateurs. In this way, the executioners made their own record of the Holocaust. Maybe you have seen the picture of the gate to Auschwitz, with its cynical slogan—"*Arbeit macht frei*," meaning, "Work sets you free." That could be the image etched in your memory. However, in hindsight, we know the most likely way out of there was through the crematory chimneys. They used various manners and methods to kill their victims: shooting, gassing, killing by poison, starvation, medical experiments, torture, and the list goes on. You see, they didn't exactly suffer from lack of ingenuity. The camera lies, as you know, but not always. Those indistinct photographs and images have one thing in common: They no longer represent humans, but what's left of them, disfigured by torture, emaciated bodies, deprived of all dignity. They represent us as humans who have lost our human worth. And that was how the Nazis made the Final Solution possible and the violence legitimate. Well, who would accuse anybody of exterminating vermin and call it murder?

Auschwitz. Chelnmo. Treblinka. Majdanek. Sobibor. These death factories, the concentration camps, were actually denied at that time until the day the Allied forces marched in. Even now, there are some people who claim these camps never really existed. They are nothing but a propaganda scam due to the lack of evidence, some say. Today Auschwitz, the largest German extermination camp, is a museum. The artifacts have been arranged somewhat in a pointless precision. You can see piles of shoes and clothes neatly sorted out in adult's and children's sections, along with bags, dentures, artificial legs, glasses, and even human hair. They all speak clearly of what kind of a reception these victims had to endure upon arrival as they were robbed of everything. There are also the death lists, carefully prepared in black and white to validate the true essence of this agony. Surely, this is evidence enough. There are still a few of us survivors left who can testify on behalf of those who didn't survive. Some of the doctors, commandants, and executioners who worked at the Nazi concentration camps have also testified about what took place behind those barbed-wire fences. We are all old now, and many have passed away, of course. At the hands of time, we are all bound to be treated equally, in the end.

My crime? Being a Jew! Bear in mind the fact this persecution didn't only affect the Jews, but it all started by terminating the physically and the mentally disabled people through euthanasia. Furthermore, as the witch hunt continued, people who considered to be of a low-standing breed, such as gypsies, Slavs, and communists, were also sent to the concentration camps. People from all kinds of different ethnic groups were incarcerated at the camps. Nazism was a racial ideology, with the Aryan race being the superior one. Religion played a subordinated role in the Third Reich.

But how could this happen? You might ask, "Is it really necessary to raise the issues of anti-Semitism and the extermination of the Jewish people once again? After all, these events happened more than seventy years ago. The perpetrators responsible for these crimes are long gone. So why bring out all the nasty memories from the past?"

The answer is simple: the evil has many faces. The hatred and the haters are still very much alive among us all. They appear in many different shapes and names, but I call them haters. The content of their views and ideas may seem unlike the old Nazis, yet if you study them closely you will recognize the resemblance, although the new generation of Nazis are careful not to mention the Final Solution. Nevertheless, they deny the Holocaust and what went on at the German concentration camps. In their opinion, these are just Jewish fabrications, and they dismiss all the facts about the camps as fictional. It is obvious to notice how the racial and anti-Semitic views are gaining more power and becoming rougher in their appearance. Those of us who have seen the growth of fascism with our own eyes can easily recognize what's going on. There are only a few harmless incidents, mostly gang fights. We hardly see any major political force threatening our democracy. And there is no sign of the rising of a Fourth Reich. But we have learned from history that it can all happen again. The hatred and the persecution have always existed, constantly evolving. To quote the historian Raul Hilberg, "The Nazi destruction process didn't come out of a void. It was the culmination of a cyclical trend. First the missionaries of Christianity had said in effect: "You have no right to live among us as Jews." The secular rulers who followed had proclaimed: You have no right to live among us. The German Nazis at last decreed: You have no right to live."

Hatred is the driving force behind all wars. Sweden is not threatened by war. The wars we must confront here are of a different kind, mostly rooted in ethnic and religious prejudice. Our ability to go through hardship and painful experiences as humans is marvelous. It took many years for my physical and psychological wounds to heal. They may not always be visible outwardly, but all Holocaust survivors have been scarred for life. But it is possible to rise from humiliation and move on. My experience has taught me to overcome anger and resentment by facing the world with tolerance and positivity. I know this for sure because of what I have been through before, during and after the war. I witnessed as a child how anti-Semitism, which at first was nothing but a silly religious misconception, grew like cancer, eating away the entire society and finally became a political doctrine. I witnessed how anti-Semitic orations grew exceedingly, gaining unlimited power. A power manifested through countless atrocities and mass murder. Ordinary decent people suddenly became hostile and blind as they were swept away by the mass psychosis that Nazism and fascism gradually created.

You might wonder if there were only fascist and Nazi supporters everywhere, and nobody stood up or protested against this collective mania. Well, of course there were people who resisted, but they did it secretly and in silence. All political resistance was obviously dangerous, and those who took part in such operations risked their lives. Even so, we should be aware of the real danger that is behind silence and passivity. Attitudes and ideas are easily converted. History repeats itself is a saying, but unfortunately it is true. What happened in Bosnia about twenty years ago is similar to what happened in Europe about seventy years ago. Even though there was no talk of the Final Solution, the Bosnian genocide was an act of ethnic cleansing. We must learn to draw conclusions from history instead of declaring all clear as soon as the storm has passed. We should be careful not to think that fascism is just a dead and forgotten part of history, and it belongs to the past. I am convinced that history is going to repeat itself as long as we do not learn from it. Therefore, I decided to write this book. I kept silent for more than fifty years, but because of the increasing level of violence around us, I consider it my duty to raise awareness and spread knowledge about Nazism and the Holocaust. It is only through relentless efforts that we are able to counteract.

I also want to shed light on and talk about the psychological mechanism that is activated when a person is cast down in deep humiliation, and what happens to a person who is completely uprooted. Parents who have suffered in their childhoods are often unaware of how those memories and experiences affect the way they raise their children. So their traumas are inherited from one generation to the next. The suffering goes on, and a vicious circle arises. Those circles can be broken.

With this book, I want to show you the power of the remarkable strength a human being has inside. How one person is able to rise from the deepest pit of degradation and still stay positive. You see, it is almost like a diamond that must be refined under heavy pressure, deep down in the heart of the mountain. A human can also be refined through their life experiences and become a positive and creative individual. This is the story of my life experiences, but it could also be the story of many who did not survive to tell theirs. I kept silent for too long, mostly because it was too painful to tell. That was the way most of them felt.

CHAPTER 2

THE IDYLL OF MY CHILDHOOD

You are probably thinking, *How was this all possible?* Well, I will try to give you some answers. So let me take you on a journey to my hometown, Velký Sevluš, in former Czechoslovakia during the 1930s. The main road went all the way up to the mountains, where all familiarity ended. My hometown lay in a contentious part of the country. This is where my story begins, right at the border between East and West, between the two wars that forever changed Europe. Before the First World War, Carpatho-Ruthenia had belonged to Austria-Hungary. After the war, it became Czech, only to become a part of Hungary again some decades later. For a short period of time, the city belonged to the Soviets, and nowadays it is Ukrainian. Who knows how the story ends. We lived in the borderland, where many different nationalities coexisted. Ukraine lay on the other side of the Carpathian chain of mountains, and it belonged to the Soviet Union. In my hometown, Velký Sevluš, there were Ruthenians and Hungarians together with Czechs. And there were Jews, of course. We were the dominant minority. When you were out and about on the streets, you could hear people speaking in various languages. We spoke Yiddish, which is a mixture of German, Hebrew, and some Polish. My Hungarian was as good as my Czech, and I could get by using Russian if I needed to. The language spoken in school was Czech. It truly was a wonderful mixture of languages and cultures. Obviously, it was quite useful being able to swear in one language and write school essays in another one. This blend of languages and the linguistic confusion caused by it could manifest itself in rather funny ways. I remember one of our neighbors had an unusually vicious dog, so they had to hang a warning sign in front of their house. The sign was written in three different languages to make sure everybody understood the fact their dog was cosmopolitan. It didn't make any difference whether it was a Greek or a Jew who passed by the house; the dog would take a bite of a Czech as well as a Russian without any hesitation.

The wineries that surrounded us had given the town its original Hungarian name, Nagy Szöllös. The old name originated from the imperial days and the Habsburgian era, meaning "the great winery." Every autumn, you could see the vines heavy with fruit at the farms along the mountainside. It was harvest time, and everybody had to help, even the kids. And we were more than happy to do so because we would earn some money—in other words, a profitable business for us. After the harvest, the winemaking process began. Everywhere you looked, you could see people trampling grapes in huge containers. Most of the time the winemakers would do this procedure with their bare feet. I am quite sure they never cared much about sanitation. I dare say they had probably been walking around in the dirt and the mud on the streets, not to mention the characteristic droppings from the horses, the pigs, and the donkeys. Perhaps this was the main reason why the wine fermented so well and became so tasty and flavorful. Even though I didn't know anything about that as a child, I simply couldn't understand why the adults drank wine.

The river Tisza, which ran right outside the town, continued its way beyond the haze of the sun, out into the unknown world, where none of us had ever been. In the south, there was Hungary, with Budapest as the capital, where one of my uncles lived. And from the United States, a continent faraway, we used to receive letters with exciting stamps. Poverty had forced many of the Eastern European Jews to emigrate to the United States at the beginning of the century. My grandfather was one of them. My mother was born in the States, but my grandmother, who never really settled there, divorced her husband, took her American-born child, and returned home. My mother was three years old then.

The world outside was not tempting to us. In fact, we were seldom reminded of its existence, except for a few occasions—the letters from the United States, for instance, which could contain the most desirable dollar bills—if we were lucky, of course. The parcels from France, where my other uncle lived, were also sought after because he always used to put some chocolate inside. The chocolate came from the factory where he worked. We were often reminded of the outside world through football tournaments that were played in exotic places, in Budapest and in other big cities in Hungary and Czechoslovakia. All the boys my age played football, and we were well aware of the famous footballers from different countries. And, of course, we all wanted to be just like them, so we trained hard. The enchanting world out there could also be found in the movies from the States. The most popular ones were Wild Westerns; they made us hungry for adventure. All the houses in our town were small, single-story wooden houses with fences. I lived in one of these houses together with my parents and four younger siblings. Our house was quite a modern one compared to the other houses in our neighborhood. We had electricity. Although they were just some dangling naked light bulbs, they spread more light than the old paraffin lamps we used to have. In the streets of the nicer parts of our town, where the ground was covered with cobblestone, life had a faster pace. There were plenty of motorbikes, horse-drawn carriages, and cabs jostling one another. A few cars, with their constant horn blowing, managed to scare people and cattle alike, but they rarely turned up.

Traveling by train to the neighboring town was an unusual adventure. As a child, I used to go down to the station to see the incoming trains. They soon departed in a cloud of steam and smell of coal smoke, leaving a tickling sensation behind. To be able to take the train and leave Velký Sevluš on a trip to visit some relatives who lived in nearby cities was my permanent wish. In my eyes, that was a great adventure. But the trains huffed away without me onboard, and I just slouched all the way home, happy I had at least seen them.

Market days were the most enjoyable ones because the Ruthenian farmers would come from the countryside, usually by foot, carrying loads of merchandise. They used to have animals on the hoof, carrying them in high stillages on their backs. The big farmers came by horse and cart. They used to pitch their stands with the merchandise, sometimes right on the ground, tightly packed in the little marketplace.

- Fat hens!
- Turnips! Potatoes! Peppers!
- Ducks! Geese!
- Eggs and fruits!
- Well-hung hares! First-rate rabbits!

The meat from the hares and the rabbits was an unfamiliar sensation to us Jews because we were not allowed to eat certain animals, according to our religion. Every salesman made sure that only he had the best products. The fattest geese and the ripest fruits. There was not only food but also clothes, carpets, and toys on sale. The market was a meeting place for everyone in town. And you had to bargain—it was part of the deal. Oftentimes you could witness people making such a fuss over the price of a melon, almost like fighting a battle. The Ruthenians were not always well mannered. During a lengthy parley with a Ruthenian farmer woman, you could suddenly hear a splashing noise. From beneath her skirts a foul stream made its way out and down to the street. There was no doubt about the contents of that puddle. No wonder why we, the city people, thought highly of ourselves when the farmers came. The commerce at the marketplace was held in many different languages, including an expressive body language. Even though sometimes it looked like a big fight was about to break out, it would turn out to be just for fun. That was the way we knew how to have a good time in Velký Sevluš.

One of the biggest market days, at the end of August, coincided with one of the major religious celebrations. It was called Bogorodica, "the Day of the Mother of God." The town square would be absolutely swarmed with people, especially toy vendors. It was almost like Christmas Eve for the kids. And since my birthday is in August, I always received plenty of gifts. I guess my sisters were quite envious of me because I was lucky enough to be born then. Another vibrant ingredient of urban life was the different religious processions. There were mostly Ruthenians out in the streets. They used to celebrate all their religious ceremonies through processions, often at the same time as the market went on. Ruthenians were Greek Orthodox.

Their version, in my opinion, was a fanatic type of religion, with many antiquated elements. Sacred icons and shrines were carried forward to the sound of murmuring prayers and monotonous chanting around the city. The procession was led by a priest, who was easily recognized due to his wide black skirts and chimneylike hat. He was followed by a group of mustachioed farmers, who were dressed in rough home-woven shirts and short boots. The women wore long skirts, often in many layers. During the summers, they walked barefoot, despite the formal occasion, followed by hordes of kids in all ages.

Most Jews and Hungarian Christians practiced and lived a more inward kind of religious life. We used to celebrate the Sabbath and other big religious ceremonies at the synagogue. Some of the bigger, more festive occasions were celebrated at homes because of the strong family ties among Jews. Our family was big. I had uncles, several cousins, and some second cousins, all living in the same town. The Jews lived everywhere in Velký Sevluš, and there were no ghettos to be found. The rabbi and the most religious people resided in the area closest to the big synagogue and around the Jewish cemetery. There was also a kosher slaughterhouse and the Jewish bakery that made the typical Sabbath bread, which is of utmost importance for the ritual supper in the evening. The Jewish religion has many regulations, considering how the food should be prepared, from the way the animals are slaughtered to which manner the food is to be ingested. Although the Jewish religion, especially back then and in Eastern Europe, had its own specific and distinctive characteristics, the Jews did not make much ado about it outwardly. The most religious Jews were quite different from the Catholics and the Greek Orthodox, simply because of their outfits. In the crowded streets, it was easy to differentiate the black and gray colors of the Orthodox. All Jewish males had to wear the little round calotte or hat because as a Jew you are not allowed to walk about with your head bare. Many of the men had corkscrew curls right by the ears, which probably looked peculiar to non-Jews.

You think this sounds like a nice idyllic small town, don't you? This all happened during the 1930s, the decade when the entire world held its breath as the optimism and hope of the 1920s was turned into depression and warmongering. The economic crisis around the world caused many people to lose their jobs, factories shut down in bankruptcy, and funds became worthless. Money had no value due to a rapidly increasing inflation. In Germany, not so far from Velký Sevluš, Hitler gained power. Life went on in our town. Nobody ever talked about politics as if the outside world hardly existed. My father who was a typographer. He worked at a printshop—the only one in the area. The town's newspaper was printed there. It came out weekly, and the content was mostly about what was going on in our town and the neighboring areas. The newspaper was bilingual, published in Hungarian and Ukrainian. World news did not have a prominent place in the paper. The official news service was done by an old man who walked the streets up and down with his drum, which was heard far around. The drum rolls called us all to follow him to the town square. There he shouted out what the authorities wanted to be said. Oftentimes it was about new rules and decrees concerning our town.

We knew very little about what happened in the rest of our country. One day it all changed. It was in the beginning of the year 1939. That day the drummer shouted out the news about our region becoming a part of Hungary. Then the old patriots who had fought during the First World War in the Hungarian army cheered in triumph. They put on their old fine uniforms from the war and proudly presented themselves with their badges of honor. There were also Jews among them who believed Hungary taking power in the region would mean a reunion with their fellow countrymen. Nobody could ever imagine that anything would happen in our remote countryside. Here peace and order would prevail forever.

CHAPTER 3

THE RISE OF ANTI-SEMITISM

Everything was not idyllic in Velký Sevluš. There was much tension and sometimes open hostility between the Ruthenians and the Jews. The Ruthenians had many inaccurate ideas about the Jews, which had their roots mainly in old religious traditions and prejudice from centuries back. In contemporary Ukraine, where the Ruthenians felt mostly related to, and in Stalin's Soviet, there were plenty of Jew haters, despite the Communist rule, which was considered to be a modern and progressive society.

Both historical and religious prejudice played their roles in Eastern Europe. I have experienced anti-Semitism as far back as I can remember. If somebody shouted, "Jew!" passing by in the street, then you had to be careful. *Jew* meant the same as "swine" or "scum." The word itself was perhaps innocent, but it was expressed in a scornful undertone that could not be mistaken. To the anti-Semite, a Jewish person was supposed to be mocked, spat on, or beaten down. A Jew has no value to the anti-Semite.

In Velký Sevluš, there were about fifteen thousand residents. The Jews were a big minority, about three thousand people.

Needless to say, not all the non-Jews who lived in our town were anti-Semites. But the Jews were quite many, and they lived all over the town. All the residents of Velký Sevluš, regardless of origin or belief, knew someone Jewish. Most of them lived under the same conditions. Nobody was particularly rich. Nobody was so successful that it would stick in the eyes of the others. We were ordinary people, living in a typical small town, and we could have been equals. And most of us felt that way firsthand. We were citizens of Sevluš and not members of a specific religion or minority.

Just like any other place, there were some bad apples in our town too—young Ruthenians with low self-esteem. The "better" citizens looked down on the Ruthenians. The pecking order was the same as in any other bully context. The strong pecks on the weak, and the defenseless become the first victims. All based on prejudice. Envy is an important driving force behind prejudice, although our life was not any different from the other citizens of Sevluš. Most Jews worked as craftsmen. Tailor, shoemaker, bricklayer, carpenter, and tinsmith were ordinary professions. Only a few had intellectual professions. There were two physicians among them. Most of us had enough, so we managed, but there were also many poor people. The Jewish community is based on providing for those who are less fortunate. The old, the sick, and the widows were all taken care of.

A great many of the Jews sympathized with communism in secret. They often thought that the communists would be able to do something about anti-Semitism. As Jews, we also hoped that the communists would fight against poverty. At that time communism still had the reputation of being a doctrine for the oppressed; therefore many people believed in a future governing labor state, where everyone had equal rights and fair living conditions. The farmers in the surrounding areas worked very hard to earn their living. Every child was supposed to attend school for at least five years, but to the farmers the schools were unnecessary. And the children who actually went to school still had to work hard and help out at the farm. Most Ruthenians were quite tough on their children. God, the teacher, and the father represented the authority, in mentioned order. Among the Ruthenian farmers, raising a child was a matter of severity and flogging. To flog a child with a belt was not a big deal. All the fathers who wanted to give their children a "decent upbringing" did that. Early on, these children learned what hatred and oppression were about. Oppression raises new tormentors. The children were fed with lies about the Jews. As soon as they could understand what the adults talked about, the persecution was there. Hatred that is imprinted at a young age is the hardest to oppose, as it is about inherited perceptions. At church, the priest preached about the crimes of the Jewish people, especially during Easter. They used to get all fired up and spiced their preaching with juicy details about how the Jews had tortured and crucified Jesus on Calvary. That was the most dangerous time of the year for a Jewish boy to walk around the town. My entire childhood was defined by this ever-present hatred and fear. To provoke or to offend someone in any way could be risky, not to mention unsafe. You had to be very careful, always on your watch and polite to strangers you met in the streets. If you were alone walking in an alley, and suddenly you saw someone, the wisest thing would be to run away. The worst case was when you didn't notice the person until you felt the bash from behind. There were plenty of tormentors.

You wonder: How can anyone understand all this? My experience is this. The sense of not having enough power may lead to an urge for gaining control by force. The often illiterate and rude famer boys could hide their sense of insecurity by flying at us, the Jews. There are almost the same mechanisms at work now as then when it comes to violent youngsters who attack foreigners, gays or black people. It is the same pattern now as it was then. In a numerically superior situation, the bully tackles the physically inferior.

Do you know about the Law of Jante? "You shall not believe that you are someone. You shall not believe that you are as good as us." We lived according to Jante. It could be dangerous to be a good student in school, or to receive compliments from the teacher could mean you were begging for punishment. Others might be jealous. I wanted to prove to myself that I was somebody! Perhaps it is typical for persecuted minorities throughout the history. On one hand, I needed to feel appreciated in order to be satisfied; on the other hand, I had to be ready to receive punishment. Appreciation on one hand and humiliation on the other hand were two sides of the same coin to me. They were somehow inevitably connected to each other.

It was absolutely forbidden to meet and socialize with non-Jewish girls. Maria was a Ruthenian girl I fancied and tried to keep company when I was fourteen years old and in love. Sometimes I took a detour passing her street. If I saw her coming together with her brother, I wouldn't even dare to look her way. He was a cocky fellow who would gladly dish out quite a wallop to a Jew if he had the chance. Maria was also interested. She invited me to her house one evening when her family was away. That was the first time I kissed a girl. Afterward I never dared to meet Maria alone again.

Family ties were extremely important due to the existing opposition in our town. The Jewish families held together.

The unity in our family was excellent. The strongest and the most essential part of the Jewish community was the family. It was my father's job to support and provide for us. I was the only son and the eldest among the siblings. That's why my father expected more of me. There was a warm atmosphere characterized by mutual trust that gave me the courage and the strength to persist the hardships of my life as a Jew. Later on, I even had strength enough to endure those horrid circumstances.

Jewish people are not necessarily strict about the matters of religion, but it is of course different from one family to the other. We were not particularly religious. My father often asked me, "You have read your prayers, haven't you?"

Naturally, I answered, "Yes, Father!" Perhaps he didn't really believe me.

One day he looked me in the eyes and said, "Do you really read your prayers?"

I nodded, trying to look innocent, but I knew something wasn't right.

My father said, "That's weird because I have put a banknote in the prayer book, and it has been there for three months, but you haven't noticed it." Then he laughed and never mentioned a word about it ever again. Or maybe it was a psychological trick to really get me to open the prayer book. Obviously, I was ashamed of myself. My parents were devout believers, and they had a close relationship to their God. We used to go to the synagogue, and I participated in the Jewish Sunday school. But none of us were fanatic or orthodox. All the Jewish families in Velký Sevluš went to the synagogue every Saturday; it was another way of fellowship. I had a good voice, and I sang in the choir, which made my father very proud. My dream was to become a musician. That dream would never come true, but that's another story.

Religion was very much about being a part of a community. After the war broke out in 1939, everything changed. Breaking the windows of the shops, trashing the Jewish graveyards and other acts of vandalism around the country, indicated that a new era was on its way. In our town, the gap between the Jews and the others became wider. As teenagers, we didn't understand much about what was going on, other than listening to the loud voices of the grown-ups. The Hungarian gendarmes shifted their attitude toward us as the Germans continued to gain power. The gendarmes had the power. They came every day wearing uniforms with feathers in the helmets and mounted, armed with whips and batons against ordinary people. The police and the gendarmes were often recruited among the farm boys of the area, and they were notorious for being brutal. They were always chasing after Jews and communists, which was the same thing to them. Raids happened frequently; they looked for forbidden books and papers for no reason. It was mostly harassment because they wanted to prove who was in charge.

We began to understand how dangerous it was to stay in Velký Sevluš. It was 1941, and we risked living under oppression and the threat of retaliation. The persecution of the Jews got worse as Hungary became a subordinate state to Germany. And we received news about the war coming closer to us. My family applied for an exit permit. Our plan was to reach the States and Grandfather. My mother was an American citizen, so as children we were considered to be Americans as well. My father managed to get his papers in order too, after some trouble, of course. Just before we were about to leave, the diplomatic relations between Hungary and the United States disrupted. The borders closed. We never made it to the United States.

CHAPTER 4

NEWS OF HORROR

The "Jew laws" were established in 1941, which implied that only 6 percent of the Jewish population were allowed to attend higher education, and also only 6 percent of the Jews were allowed to have businesses of their own. Among the upper classes in Hungary, there were major estate owners, corporate leaders and intellectuals of Jewish descent. Their influence obstructed the worst persecution for a while. In 1941 their position began to disintegrate but those 6 percent were basically the same as the wealthiest Jews in the society. The Jew laws affected the majority, the most vulnerable the worst. Our position was threatened, but yet we managed to get by without having to wear the Star of David, the six-pointed yellow star with the word *Jew*. We could still live relatively free, for some time. But the war was getting significantly closer.

During the war years, we had less and less to eat. The printshop was short of work, and the coin rolls that my father received as salary shrank in more than one way. The rationing, the higher food prices and the inflation decreased the value of the money we had. Sometimes the food was completely deficient. My father's cousin had a pub not far from our house. The farmers used to gather there to chat and gossip over a simple meal and a few shots of liquor. My mother sent me there to fetch some food on credit, an assignment I absolutely loathed. But the bread and the smoked fish, served at the pub, were satisfactory. The pub was a meeting place for the people who were on the road. Here you could receive some news about the world outside our end of country. I met Jewish refugees from the ghetto in Warsaw for the first time at the pub. They had taken a huge risk escaping the heavily guarded ghetto. Those of us who gathered around these exhausted and skinny men, listened ever more curious with increasing fear. After the Germans took over the power, the Schutzstaffel (SS) had gathered all the surviving Jews in the ghetto in Warsaw. More than six hundred thousand people lived there. The ghetto was accommodated in a few blocks, surrounded by high walls. Here people died in the streets either of disease or of starvation. Dead bodies lay everywhere. The abandoned and the old were looking for some leftovers in the garbage bins in order to survive just another day. The German SS found it amusing to shoot the dot at Jews and call it "attempted escape."

The stories about epidemics, starvation, torture, and killings were new to us. We didn't know what to believe. Was it the figment of imagination? Or at least rough exaggerations? It was difficult for us to believe them. The truth, we neither dared to think of nor could grasp was this, those stories would become reality the moment the German terror reached all of us. And the ghetto in Warsaw was some sort of a prototype for the other ghettos that we soon would see all around us, even in the remote Velký Sevluš. During the summer of 1942, I was considered to be an almost grown young man, by the life standard back then. I had to start providing for myself. There were no opportunities back home. My uncle lived in Budapest, and he promised to take care of me. All railways in Hungary lead to Budapest. I was sixteen years old when I, for the first time, lost and shy, came to that elegant railway station. More than one million people lived in Budapest who walked about in those broad boulevards in an urbane and quite blunt manner, without even casting an eye at a hillbilly like me. Budapest was a faceless city just like any other big city. People from different nationalities and ethnical minorities lived together side by side in harmony. Being Jewish or Ruthenian didn't matter in this case, as long as you blended in among the other residents. So I quickly slipped the calotte into my pocket. Maybe I was a bit ashamed, since it was considered a great sin going about bareheaded, according to the Jewish custom. I wouldn't dare to think of what my father had said if he had seen me there and then, but nobody knew who I was.

Back then Budapest was an international metropole. There was a constant overflow of different types of music everywhere. My cousin and I used to walk down the boulevards evenings on end. She was a beautiful and confident girl who studied piano and song at the music conservatory. You could hear the music everywhere coming out of the tearooms and the bars. At luxurious night clubs, such as Moulin Rouge and the Amazona bar, there was a sophisticated upper-class drinking and dancing. The entertainment offered at the theaters was bold and politically provocative, disguised as burlesque. The cinemas located next to each other showed American movies, which were my favorites. I was always craving for sweets. From the tearooms with exotic names, such as New York and Japan, you could sense the tempting aroma of a special kind of a pastry with poppy seeds that I just could not resist, as long as I had some money in my pocket. Perhaps there was yet another Budapest than the one I met during my walks in early mornings and late evenings. There was not much evidence of the existing war. I never heard people discussing politics. I watched jovial wage earners dressed in overalls rushing to and forth their jobs. I watched serious-looking, neatly dressed clerks jostling one another at the barbershops. Peace and order ruled everywhere. On the famous bridges of Budapest, at the Dunacorso, the elegant beach walk, at the zoo and in the fashionable city parks, you could see the well-dressed residents of Budapest strolling about lazily and seemingly without any concerns whatsoever. There was no lack of stocks in the major stores. In Budapest, you could buy anything at the black market, even exclusive products, such as French cognac and Russian caviar. Nobody suffered so to speak, at least not as long as you had money.

The only thing reminding you of the war was the fact you could see heavily armed gendarmes and mounted police patrolling down the boulevards. There weren't many jobs for a young boy from country. I started working as an errand boy at a tailor shop. The tailor had a reputation of being terribly stingy, with a fiery temper. Now, it didn't bother me, because I had been brought up to be polite and observant. His stinginess became obvious to me when it was time for the weekly bath. As the master stepped out of his bath, the soap made the water milky white but there were thick stripes of dirt floating on the sides of the tub. No doubt he wouldn't warm up a fresh bucket of water for the apprentice, so I just had to get in the same bathwater. I didn't receive any salary other than the tips the customers gave me when I delivered their clothes. I was offered food and lodging, as was the custom in those days.

Budapest was a safe haven. The feeling of serenity turned out to be deceptive. The war was getting closer and closer. At the Eastern front, the German army was struggling, and their setbacks kept coming, one after the other. Both the German and the Russian armies were getting closer to our borders. The air raids began by this time. The alerts were heard daily, and as the bombs fell we had to run down to the shelters. The war we had tried to avoid moved closer and closer each day. People in Hungary were just as afraid of the Red Army as the German Wehrmacht. Also, back home, people began to feel anxious. I received a letter from my father, pleading for my homecoming. In Nagy Szöllös, as the city was called now after becoming Hungarian, father believed we would be protected by the mountains from the threatening war. Reluctantly, I returned home. Until 1944, Hungary had been ruled by the German-friendly, though, in the Third Reich's opinion, unreliable Admiral Horthy. The most extreme manifestations of Nazism had never reached Hungary, because of Horthy's claim on certain democratic rights.

There was a radical fascist movement, outright anti-Semitic and antidemocratic, called the Arrow Cross. The reason they called themselves that was the black-red-white symbol found on their armlets and flags, the arrow cross. Their recruits were among young men with a weapon fixation, often criminals, alcoholics, or outcasts. They often gathered in large groups, ravaging about on the streets and allies. They pulled their guns or knives recklessly at anyone they didn't like, even non-Jews. They were amused by torturing people as real sadists. One of their more spectacular methods was push-ups. First they would catch someone. By beating and kicking the victim, he was forced to the ground. They placed an erect knife right under the victim's body. When he could no longer continue doing the push-ups, his body was penetrated by the knife. Such events were typical for the members of the Arrow Cross. Their political ideal was open terror—an "ideology" that was rooted in contempt for the weak.

On March 19, 1944, the Nazis invaded Hungary. The former government was removed from office. Several eminent politicians, dignitaries and industry managers were imprisoned the same day. Germans and members of the arrow cross gained unlimited power. Thereby, there were no restrictions against the Nazi's rule of terror. It was time for the Final Solution in Hungary. A task force under Adolf Eichmann's command was put in charge of implementing the deportations. At this time there were eight hundred thousand Jews living in the country, about two hundred thousand only in Budapest. About a week after the German invasion, it was announced that all Jews had to wear the six-pointed yellow Star of David. The terror accelerated rapidly. New Jew-laws were established gradually. Jewish properties were confiscated. Jews were no longer allowed to practice their professions. Jews were forbidden to visit restaurants and cinemas. Jews were not allowed to sit on park benches. Not to travel by train or car. So on. The list could be longer. After a few weeks, new ghettos were set up all over the country, the last stop to Auschwitz. The long line of freight trains started toward the extermination camps, day and night. Eichmann proved to be both zealous and efficient. Between May 15 and July 7, six hundred thousand Jews were transported to Auschwitz. They were mostly from the Hungarian countryside, where the Jewish population was practically wiped out. A dreadful ghetto was set up in Budapest similar to the one in Warsaw, a death camp. Only a few survived.

CHAPTER 5

OUR HOME IN THE GHETTO

The drummer came to our town as usual and announced the new decrees. All Jews had to wear the Star of David. About a week later, there was yet another order: the Jews had to leave their homes. We were moved to a temporary ghetto. Some gendarmes from our neighborhood came to our house. They delivered meticulous instructions about what we should pack. Thereafter, the house was under their watch. Stealthily, I managed to hide an alarm clock. In a time of poverty and destitution, it was a true luxury. I didn't want to see my alarm clock in the hands of the gendarmes; therefore I sneaked out and buried it in our garden. I was totally convinced we would soon be back home. As my family stood lined up with our luggage, the gendarmes started to nail the doors and the windows with planks. "No one would enter the vacated house," they said. I still remember the hammer blows, triumphantly thinking of the alarm clock that wouldn't be theirs. None in the family could even imagine us not returning to our home. The hastily set up ghetto was located on the same street as the synagogue, the cemetery, and the kosher slaughterhouse. The small, low houses along that street had housed about two hundred people. Now all the Jews of the town were supposed to lodge in there. In every room, there were about twenty people. People who didn't really even know each other that well were forced to live together. Among us, there were fussy children, old and sick people who all needed peace and quiet.

It was spring and still cold. There were neither deliveries of firewood nor food to the ghetto. We sat cowering, shivering on the floor and tried to keep warm. Due to the lack of water, it was impossible to wash clothes or to keep ourselves clean. The smell of sweat and urine, the filth, it all became worse when the spring arrived. In our regions, it could get quite warm. Many of the old and the sick complained constantly. We tried to comfort them, often in vain. Sometimes there is no cure for despair. There were two physicians in the ghetto. They had neither instruments nor medicine. Perhaps what was worst was not the dirt or the congestion but the state of uncertainty. Many people became more and more apathetic, they almost didn't speak at all. For us, as young men, there was a break in the monotony. Our responsibility was to make sure that nobody escaped, which in fact was quite a meaningless guard-duty. On the other side of the crafted fence, there were gendarmes patrolling with their heavy-loaded guns, so the chance to get away was nonexistent.

Four weeks passed or maybe more. It felt as if time had ceased to exist. One day we received order for departure. By whipping and threatening with pointed guns, the gendarmes managed to move us toward the synagogue. There wasn't enough room for everyone. Outside the synagogue, there was a blind alley. Those who were pushed in the already packed synagogue, got stuck in between as the gendarmes kept pressing people in from the other side of the alley. A German uniformed SS officer, or as the Nazis called it "an expert on Jew issues," walked around with a whip in one hand and a gun in the other one. Panic broke out. To make matters even worse, the SS officer went about lashing at the crowd with his whip. He treated the old and the women the hardest. It was as if he intentionally wanted to cause as much harm as possible and made sure the bleeding people were visible. The crowd acted like frightened cattle. Many lost their family members in the turmoil. Terrified children were crying for their mothers and the mothers for their children. We were about to be registered, but this was only a meaningless formality. The registration was part of the big fraud the German Nazis orchestrated to disguise the real intention behind the deportations. The officers sat at long wooden tables with their questionnaires. Most of them were ordinary people, Sevluš citizens, and many of them were acquainted with my father. One of them was an old regular customer at my father's printshop. "What is going to happen to us?" my father asked.

"A work camp," the officer replied. He assured us that we would come back. Even today, I am totally convinced he truly believed he was telling the truth. The Germans had never revealed their actual plans to those who handled the registration in order to avoid rumors and thereby possible riots. This was part of the Nazi scheme—to make people live under threat and suspense. Threat to scare us to obedience. Suspense was a more refined instrument. Suspense could mean hope of something better awaiting us. The combination worked perfectly. Nobody dared to protest but to adapt and not grumble. As the victims of Nazism, we realized the truth far too late. After the registration, we were told to move toward the train station. The streets were crowded with people, among them several of those who used to harass us and call us "Jew bastards" and torment us in the dark. I really hoped that many of those who saw us marching toward the train station at the point of the guns, would feel ashamed. The way to the station was past the square. Here they had raised gallows to hang six people who were suspected communists. There were two Jews among them. The bodies were still hanging in their gallows. They had not been cut down in order to serve as a warning. This was the last thing I saw in Velký Sevluš before we reached the train station. The silent crowd alongside the streets. The bodies hanging as a reminder of what happened to the insurgent. We pressed anxiously toward each other and tried not to draw attention to ourselves as the SS officer kept on charging us forward with his whip. At the same time, we tried to cheer each other up. After all, it was only a working camp.

At the station, there was a long train with wagons, same kind of wagons as used for cattle transportations. Approximately sixty people were squeezed in each wagon that would actually contain about half the size. In one corner of the wagon, there was a huge bucket. That was our toilet. The men tried to pee through a crack by the door. They lined up there. When it was my turn, I could not pee so much as a single drop. I had pushed myself out of shame for so long that I no longer could pee. The pain became almost unbearable. That's what I remember above all. The pain and the shame. We traveled day and night. Sometimes fast, sometimes the train slowed down in order to halt. Once or twice, new wagons were connected. We didn't know anything about where we were going or how long it would take to reach the destination. In our wagon, there was a little barred hatch. We could only perceive the shifting of day and night, it helped us to sense the passing of time. Suddenly the train stopped at a large station, and I managed to get a glimpse through the hatch. I saw signs in Czech. And I heard voices from outside. Hands holding pieces of bread and apples reached out to us through the chinks. These people probably risked their lives for our sake. That was the only time during our journey we actually had a close encounter with the outside world. Every now and then the train halted suddenly and made unexpected stops. Under harsh surveillance, we were allowed to drain the overfull latrine bucket, though we were unable to make any conclusions about our location by looking at the desolate surroundings. Nightmares usually stop as soon as you wake up, but our journey just went on, seemingly with no end. After the war was over, we were told that sometimes they just sent the trains round and round for weeks on end at random to make sure people died during the transport.

The horrible smell in the wagon became unendurable. We ran out of the food we had shared in the beginning. The water as well. The sick and the old got worse. The death agony went on for several hours. You could hear their breaths becoming shorter and more strained. Eventually, the last breath was heard, and then it was total silence. Later on we learned the exact same scene had been repeated in all the other wagons too. The weakest died, and babies were born. At last the train stopped. The sealed doors were opened. "*Raus*! *Raus*! *Schneller*! *Los*!" the German officers roared out their orders. Nothing was fast enough to them. Some were pushed down to the ground just because they were too slow. We had reached our destination: Auschwitz-Birkenau.

CHAPTER 6

RESISTANCE MEANT SUICIDE

The trains often arrived during the night. In the dead of night, the watchtowers appeared somewhat unreal, as in a movie scene. The glowing spotlights emphasized the theatrical, but the trained dogs that attacked humans on command, as well as the loaded rifles and the officers, spoke a different kind of language—an unimaginable and horrifying reality.

Our transport arrived in the daylight. Our carefully packed suitcases were all thrown in a pile, some of them cracked open as they hit the ground. Those who were bold enough to try and save some of their valuable belongings were brutally driven away by the guards. We would never see our luggage ever again. We still didn't know anything about what was awaiting us as we were rushed out of the trains. The first sorting out, or the selection, as it was called, happened here. The soldiers looked very menacing all along. They commanded us to line up in two separate rows, men in one, women and children in the other. Soldiers with dogs urged on. People started to panic. Many cried. Any sign that could be interpreted as an attempt to resist would be punished by shooting. An old man was shot down right in front of me.

We were scared and exhausted. In that moment, resistance was the same as suicide.

Perhaps we still hoped that the nightmare wouldn't turn out to be true, that somehow it would soon be over. I wonder if we still put our trust in the explanations we received at the registration by the synagogue. Maybe this was just a work camp after all. Afterward it was hard to understand. Somebody doubted the vague promises and started talking to the others. The guards didn't actually deny the fact we were in a work camp. We were told we were going to take a shower and be disinfected, have some rest and some food to eat, if we behaved well enough, of course. Needless to say, it was just a well-directed act. None of those who started that designated death walk were sure about what to expect until the doors to the gas chambers were locked.

There were Polish Jews among those who took care of the reception. As we learned later on, they had been deported to Auschwitz a few years earlier. We stared at them. They were assistance prisoners, all dressed in the typical striped uniform. Who were they? Were they really Jews like us? Some of the older prisoners tried to give us information about where we were. "This is a death camp!" they told us. And also about the gas chambers and all the cruelties that went on in the camp. Not even then could we believe them, although it all scared us. We lined up in long rows. Those who were estimated to be useful as manpower would get to live. I was nineteen, young and strong, capable of labor. The line started to move forward. Slowly we passed by a man, dressed in an SS uniform, just like all the other ones, but he was surrounded by a notable air of elegance. He stood completely still on a platform, with a whip in his hand, and he observed the passersby with an icy, straight look upon his face. He ordered whether a prisoner would go to the right or to the left just by making small gestures. This was Doctor Mengele, subsequently one of the most notorious criminals in Nazi Germany. The man who was responsible for the monstrous medical experiments in Auschwitz. The man behind the selection in Auschwitz. A murderer. In just a few seconds, he gave his verdict and decided who was healthy and able-bodied and would get to live.

Even though we didn't quite understand what was going on, we had a feeling he had the power over life and death. We noticed that the old and the sick were instructed to the right line. Everybody tried to straighten up for a moment as we passed by Doctor Mengele's eyes. My father limped slightly on one foot due to an old injury from the First World War so, he grabbed my arm tightly as we passed by the executioner together. My mother and my four sisters stood in another line about three meters away from us. We could see each other for a moment before the lines started to move. Mengele took a look at my father and me, gave the sign, and pointed to the left line, the one leading to the work camp. We would get to live. My mother and my two youngest sisters, who were ten and twelve years old, were assigned to the line with gas chambers and crematories as destination. My two older sisters, who were fifteen and seventeen years old, ended up among those who would work, and thereby received a short respite from death. A few lucky ones survived the camp. My sister Elisabeth was one of them. We were reunited after the war. In that short moment in front of Mengele, my entire family's fate was determined.

The long line of people who patiently marched toward the gas chambers and the crematories could probably understand that something wasn't right, judging by the thick yellowish smoke and the sweetish stench surrounding them. Some of the weakest ones were offered a ride, which they thought was a Red Cross ambulance, all in order to prevent panic. The march toward the gas chambers went by the nicely raked gravel walkways. They were surrounded by beautiful beds of flowers. The chambers were hidden behind the bushes. Perhaps they had been inspired by the many popular health resorts from the area. The death factory was an idyll in disguise. My mother and my two young siblings disappeared in the crowd. My father and I saw them for a brief moment as the right line started to move and passed by the flat muddy plain against the mounds of barracks and the pungent smell. We would never see them again.

CHAPTER 7

MY NAME BECAME A NUMBER

"*Vorwärts!*" The left line of men was commended to march forward. We were transferred to open sheds functioning as some kind of an intake section where we were deprived of whatever that reminded us of normal, ordinary life. First thing on the list was haircut and shaving, and it was all done rapidly by some of the older service prisoners. The scissors and the tools they used weren't exactly sharpened, so it really hurt. One might think they did this because of sanitary reasons. But a more weighing reason was, of course, that they wanted us to lose our personalities. Besides, a prisoner like that was easily recognized if he tried to escape. In order to emphasize our collective identity as prisoners even more, a four-centimeter broad stripe was left on the top of the head. Second on the list was shower and disinfection—namely, a cold shower and cleansing with a coarse soap. The disinfectant consisted of a blue, very fragrant liquid that was sprinkled on us. Our clothes were confiscated, except for the shoes because there was a lack of them. This was a privilege to my father since his shoes were especially made for him due to his foot injury. Normally all prisoners had heavy clogs.

The Kapon, a prisoner who had a commanding position in relation to other prisoners and cooperated with the camp leadership, threw us one pair of underwear, one pair of trousers, one shirt and one pair of socks, the outer garments were striped according to the local fashion. The prison clothes were ours to keep until they fell off, no change of clothes was offered. As outerwear, we used a jacket and a garrison-cap. During the summer, it sufficed. But in the winter, it would mean that most of us got frostbitten, at least in some body part since no extra clothes were handed out. Washing our clothes was almost impossible. Once in a while we were offered access to warm water. The water was supposed to be enough for both our laundry and our personal hygiene; therefore our clothes always came second.

Tattooing a number on the left forearm was part of the reception procedure. With carelessly cleaned tattoo needles and smeared ink, one's position was established: the camp prisoner. But the famous German efficiency had its gaps. As too many transports arrived at the same time, the Germans couldn't keep up their routines due to a lack of time. There appeared to be such haste upon our arrival. The tattooists simply couldn't cope with the pace. My group only received one of those mandatory pieces of cloth with a number on it, to attach, well visible, on our jackets. We no longer had a name. Prisoners were addressed only by their numbers. By the end of the procedure, we were commanded to line up outside, and the Kapon gave the order to march forward. After marching a while, we came to our block.

Auschwitz-Birkenau was a combined work and extermination camp. The work camp consisted of identical barracks, with room for about sixty prisoners each. On the paper, there was space for sixty thousand prisoners. In reality, there were significantly more. Our overcrowded accommodations had some kind of a grotesque expression about them—sometimes you could see a one-man bunk hold up to six prisoners. The furnishing was utterly meager and consisted of a fireplace surrounded by bunks in three floors. On the bottom, the bunks were covered with foul-smelling straw, and we only had a thin blanket to cover us with when it was cold. Our group stayed at Birkenau for about four weeks. Around us, there was an on-going selection all the time. At first we thought the selection was about different kinds of work but eventually we began to realize what the Polish Jews had told us in the beginning was true. Those who were considered expendables or affected by illness in the work camp were transferred to the gas chambers. The selection was ongoing. We were constantly reminded of what kind of a place Birkenau was by the pungent smoke and the sweet, nauseating smell.

Concentration camps had existed in Germany since the mid-1930s. These camps had been set up in order to imprison political opponents and dissidents for timeless punishment as political education. After the Wannsee Conference in 1942, when the Nazis defined the guidelines for the Final Solution, the concentration camps played a new role: to mainly function as extermination camps. Many of the large extermination camps were located in the east, in southern Poland. Even though there were camps all over the German Reich, which covered a much larger territory than now, the largest one was Auschwitz. According to the official death statistics, 1.5 million people were killed in Auschwitz-Birkenau. *Auschwitz* was some sort of an umbrella term, a center for about forty different camps, all executively subordinate to the head camp. It was located outside a town in inaccessible areas in southern Poland, where many of the inhabitants were somehow involved in the camp. Here you could find train crew, physicians and solicitors, a large number of technicians for factories, and service providers for the crematories, in addition to SS and private soldiers. Some of the largest factories in Germany had branches there, including IG Farben, Siemens, and Krupp. All slave labor carried out by the camp prisoners. Slave workers were found in all the minor camps surrounding the main camp.

This would be our fate. As newcomers, we were quartered in our own barracks. They didn't want us to socialize with the other prisoners. The only other prisoners we had any contact with were the so-called Kapos. As mentioned before, Kapos cooperated with the camp staff out of mere survival reasons. After a while, though, many of them had lost any sense of morality or respect for their fellow humans. They became tormentors. The days passed slowly. The only interruption was when we were commanded to the call site (*appellplatz*) to be counted, which occurred morning and evening. There was also daily selection. The uncertainty was gruesome. Who was going to be taken away the next day? But more than anything else, it was the idleness that tormented us. It felt like vacation in hell. After a few weeks, the Kapos asked if there were any skilled people with experience in blasting tunnels and lying rails. There was a lack of workers on the railway construction site. In fact, none of us had any such experience at all, but we were picked out anyway. We were transported in trucks to a smaller camp outside the territory of Auschwitz to a work camp called Dernau. The selection was a relief. We were granted a reprieve, and Dernau was a real work camp. It is said that hope is the thing with feathers. And the hope of a more bearable existence kept us alive. Perhaps work would give us the freedom that was promised, as the motto at the entrance of Auschwitz suggested.

CHAPTER 8

WHY THIS CRUELTY?

Dernau was one of the smaller work camps. It was isolated in the countryside, located in an area called Lower Silesia, near the town of Breslau. We didn't have much contact with the surrounding camps. The work we were assigned to do was classified. We were part of a team that was supposed to work with blasting for the construction of a tunnel. We were prepared for hard work but not for maltreatment. Neither were we prepared for the constant punishments for disregarded wrongdoings, which was part of the humiliation in order to force us to toe the line. "*Sauhund*! Swine dog!" That was the common word of speech at Dernau.

The commandant was called Wolf. He was a true sadist. He never parted from his long and heavy cudgel. I can still see his face in front of me today. His skin was very pale. He literally chewed froth, a string of foam always pushed out of the corner of his mouth. Staring gaze like a mentally ill person. All the SS men had their own favorite methods of torture. One specialty was to hit the kidneys. Another was against the genitals. A third one hit the carotids. That strike only needed to be carried out once. Wolf preferred to aim for the head and the feet. The only creature Wolf showed some kind of affection to, was his German shepherd dog.

All the days were basically alike. We had to wake up at five o'clock in the morning, except for Sunday, which was the only free day of the week. First we had to go through the whole morning procedure: half an hour to get dressed, go to the toilet, and have some breakfast, unless the call was delayed. Going to the toilet was a real torture. The camp was equipped with a large latrine pit with bars around it. You had to crawl up and hold on tight like a hen on a stick. Before and after the breakfast, there was the lineup at the call site. All the prisoners were expected to stand firm at attention as the commandant passed by. Somebody was always flogged right there and then. Mostly for no reason at all. Somehow the order of the camp was based on random punishment. But to make the punishment more efficient, the rule "one for all, all for one" was applied. The prisoner who had committed an offense had to share his punishment with the others. For this reason, we all did our very best to maintain the discipline, not to evoke our fellow prisoners' annoyance.

The methods of punishment varied, and they made a great effort of ingenuity to invent new ways. One method was the physical exercise each morning. We had to do push-ups and knee-bows, accompanied by lashes until one couldn't stand anymore and fell down in exhaustion. This was especially painful for my father, who wasn't always fast enough to react because of his injured foot. As a result, he didn't manage to perform these exercises so well, which annoyed the guards, who didn't care about the elderly or the disabled whatsoever. The one who wasn't efficient enough was always punished, as he was considered either lazy or disobedient. Another method was to stand up straight at the call site with our backs turned against the guards, who sat comfortably inside the barracks. We stood there like that for hours, regardless of the weather. Anyone who moved received an extra round of beatings. A devilish trick was that we never knew whether they were watching us or not. The guards kept out of sight. If the SS men weren't in the mood to come up with some new devilry, or if they had enough for one day, then the breakfast would be handed out. It consisted of disgusting-flavored coffee and one piece of bread. The bread that was served was peculiarly dark, flinty, and tasteless, as if it was made with bone flour. The bread ration was about ten centimeters long and five centimeters thick. And it was supposed to be sufficient for a whole day. We took small, tiny bites of the bread so it would last longer. The coffee was essential. We always froze since we were hungry all the time. That scalding, disgusting slurry kept us warm.

The workday started with a mile-long march to the tunnel in a fast pace, accompanied by breathless singing. That was an order, to sing. If ordinary people observed us on the way, we would appear to be full of joy, in a good mood, lacking nothing at all. We worked under surveillance of armed soldiers. Those who didn't do their job or misbehaved would be reported to Wolf in the evening. The soldiers carefully watched every move we made, even visiting the toilet. Here there was an outhouse for one hundred people. You could only stay for five minutes before they pushed you away, no matter if you were done or not. Since we all suffered from chronic diarrhea after a while, it was considered a benefit to be able to visit the latrine pit. Obviously, the guards noticed that and used it either as a punishment or as a reward, whichever way they pleased. Freedom and death were apparently the same according to the special logic of Nazism.

The risk of getting killed during the work was huge. To handle explosives in construction work is risky in all circumstances. In our team, there was no experienced blaster. No safety precautions existed. Not even a warning signal before a blast went off. Worst of all for those who worked inside the tunnel. Accidents often occurred. Once, twelve prisoners were killed. Four survived with severe skull injuries though. There were no paramedics to take care of them. They had to wait outside the construction area, lying on the ground, until the workday was over. We didn't have any stretchers, but we carried them back to the camp. There were neither doctors nor medicine to take care of the wounds, only some ointment and primitive aid kits. Those with minor injuries managed to live for a few hours, maybe even a few days. But they all died after suffering in vain. I was one of those who had to carry out their badly mangled bodies to the gathering point for corpses. It was the first time I had to hold a dead body with my own hands. I felt sick and did my best to avoid it. I even tried to buy myself out of it with some cigarettes, but unfortunately I couldn't get away.

My father and I were appointed the task of taking care of the rocks after the blasting. We had to use sledgehammers to smash the bigger rocks and then carry the pieces to railway wagons. The job was awfully heavy, and our hands were torn, carrying those sharp rocks without any tools. Somehow, I managed quite well but it was terribly hard for my father to cope with the fast pace. We worked up to twelve hours before it was time to march back to the camp. The elderly struggled and so did my father. I did my best to support him although it was a heavy burden. As soon as we came back to the camp, we had to lineup and report. Wolf always found something to get his teeth into. The penalties followed, depending on his mood. To stand naked in a barrel with cold water was one of the more popular penalties. A young boy had to do that one night for no reason. The following morning, he was instructed to run toward the barbed wires. To do such a thing was considered attempted escape, with the penalty being death. Wolf tried to force him to run so that he could easily shoot the poor boy on the spot. The boy refused and managed to get away, but he was beaten up, of course.

Any attempted escape was a possible way to commit suicide, for the prisoners who could no longer stand it anymore. Sometimes it was arranged. The SS man who shot a prisoner on the run, was rewarded with cigarettes or some liquor. Every now and then the SS men shot people who allegedly attempted to escape, just to cash in their reward. Cigarettes and liquor were highly coveted, and a camp prisoner's life had no worth.

When the evening call (*appellen*) was completed, the supper was handed out. Usually some kind of a soup made of bad potatoes and some other undefined ingredients. Whatever it was, we ate it with voracious appetite. The food was a chapter in itself. The most common cause of death in workcamps, was simply lack of food and starvation. Hunger was part of the repression—that is, the control over us. On the one hand, they gave us so much food that we would survive a few months. The average lifespan of a prisoner was three to four months. On the other hand, they used it in a cunning manner to keep us calm. Hunger causes apathy. You lose the ability to concentrate and the capacity to remember. Apathetic prisoners don't revolt. After the supper, we were back in the barracks. We had nothing to do, during the evenings. We were constantly plagued by lice and our only hobby, was to sit naked and pick lice like monkeys. In a certain sense, I was privileged. I could talk to my father who despite the hardship and his bad shape, managed to lift himself up. The thought of death didn't scare him. He kept his secret resistance in a diary that was lost with him when he died. Somehow, he had managed to find some paper and a blunt aniline pen. Every night, he wrote in his little book. He never let me read though. Perhaps he wrote the same story I am telling you now.

The summer passed, and a cool and humid autumn began. Statistically, we could survive until the winter came. We were constantly confronted with death. Right outside our camp there was a gathering point for corpses. New transports arrived daily, from nearby camps. The pile mounted up all the time. The summer heat caused tons of flies to buzz around them. The bodies swelled in the heat and the hard-working flies hastened the process of decomposition. I don't know why they didn't bother to bury the dead. Perhaps there weren't enough people to take care of the dead since we found ourselves at the final stage of the war, and many died. This view gave me nightmares for many years to come. The smell of the corpses. The expressions on their faces. The emaciated and humiliated bodies. Yet there was still hope. We knew that the Germans would lose the war. We noticed, during the autumn, how anxious the SS men became. It was just a matter of time. The aggressivity toward us increased with their defeats. The cruelties accelerated, many were shot or tortured to death for mere trifles. A young errand boy who worked in the kitchen and was assigned to peel the potatoes was ordered to stand naked in front of us. His was charged with stealing some potato peel from the kitchen. The Germans used the potato peel to feed the pigs, so stealing the peel was a punishable offense. The pigs were more important than the prisoners. Among the prisoners, this potato peel was a trading currency. Nonsmokers traded cigarettes for some potato peel. The boy was brutally beaten by the commandant. Other prisoners were instructed to put him in a barrel filled with ice-cold water. He spent two days and nights in there. He was supposed to freeze to death. Oddly enough, he survived. The will to live is a powerful force.

CHAPTER 9

SETBACK FOR THE GERMANS

A few months later, my father and I were transferred together with a group of prisoners from Dernau to another camp close by. The camp was under the same command. We continued working in the tunnel laying the rails. Late autumn was cold. We froze terribly in our thin clothes. The heat in the tunnel and the shift of the temperature at the lineups was the main reason many of us caught a cold constantly. And this camp had a sadistic commandant too.

The German setbacks became more and more obvious. The food got even worse, with no nutrition whatsoever. You could find all kinds of things floating around in the soup, pieces of paper and sawdust in a muddy broth. Many swelled up and were taken with dysentery. That constant diarrhea became a plague for all of us. The diseases changed our appearances, we looked more like the living dead. Many had swollen feet, they looked like elephant feet.

Terror and despair did leave a mark. Even the very young looked very old. A young boy became hoary overnight. Not everybody had given up just yet. Two young boys managed to escape and hid away for three days in hope of finding the Allies and thereby freedom. Fugitives were not heard of. The risk of getting caught was almost 100 percent. Civilian clothes were not easy to find. So, to keep out of sight for some time, in rural areas wearing the prison clothes, was impossible. That's why the camps were escape-proof. Those who against all odds made an attempt were executed.

Naturally, the fugitives were caught and brought back to the camp. It was important to set an example. The commandant's prestige was at stake. The hanging was prepared meticulously. Two brand new gallows were set up at the call site. The commandants from all nearby camps were invited. The esteemed guests were offered to sit at the especially arranged seating area for the spectators. The prisoners had to stand in a circle around the hanging site, forced to watch the execution. In order to teach us a lesson, the hanging was executed by fellow prisoners. Nobody volunteered freely. But somebody had to do it. Finally, our Kapo, a fellow prisoner also the foreman chosen by the Nazis, had to execute the order. The two boys were taken to the gallows and the ropes were wrapped around their necks. The commandant spoke about justice and lawful punishment. And the punishment that awaited those who would attempt to flee, in the future. After his speech, the commandant gave a signal. The first hanging was quickly over. The dead body was cut down and taken inside the adjacent shed that functioned as a provisional morgue, until further transport to a nearby mass grave or the like.

Next hanging was more complicated and above all macabre. When the box that the boy stood on was kicked aside, the rope went off. The boy crawled all the way to the commandant's boots and begged for mercy. The commandant kicked him in the face and ordered double ropes for the next round.

This time the executioner succeeded. A doctor, also a fellow prisoner, examined the body and stated death by cardiac arrest. This boy, too, was carried inside the shed. The commandant continued his speech. Suddenly some distinctive noise was heard from the shed. As if somebody was suffocating. The boy was still alive. We saw how the commandant reached for his gun and stared at the doctor to put the blame on him for the failed hanging. The deputy commandant, who had shown slightly human behavior on some occasions, ran inside. A shot was heard. The sound of the exhalation and gasping for air recurred. The boy was still alive. So another shot was heard. Then all went silent. This particular incident deeply touched us all, even though we were quite used to such events. The deputy commandant's intervention extinguished one life and saved another, the doctor's.

Not only the escape attempts and petty thefts were punished but also anything that could be a sign of rebellion. If there was a group gathering, it might indicate conspiracy. Therefore, it was forbidden to make conversations in groups. One Sunday a few prisoners had stopped by outside our barrack. Disperse the crowd, the commandant shouted as he was passing by. Maybe we weren't fast enough. All of a sudden, he stood there, holding an axe. He started to swing it and let it hit at random. Many skulls were ruptured. Luckily, I stood out of sight, but I was absolutely petrified.

The commandant appeared to have some unexpected traits of character. Sadly, I find it hard to believe that it was about compassion. He noticed that my father was a diligent and orderly man. Cleaning help was needed at the camp, someone who could keep things in order in the barracks. The work was much easier than the tunnel work. So my father was put in charge of the cleaning. This meant that he didn't have to march back and forth to the tunnel construction site. Probably that was the reason he survived the winter. Later on, they needed help with mopping the floors. I was chosen for the work. Unfortunately, I cut my finger on a rusty nail. An infection was inevitable since I wasn't able to wash the wound properly. I hoped that I would receive some sort of a reward for doing such an excellent job. I remained by the door. The soldier supervising the whole thing pretended not to see me at first. After a while, he looked at me and said: get lost, why are you standing there, doing nothing?

Cigarettes were sought after among the prisoners as well. At the construction site, the soldiers often had nothing to do, except to keep watch and smoke. A popular and amusing game they played, was to throw away a burning cigarette butt, near a prisoner. If the prisoner made an attempt to reach for the tempting cigarette butt, the soldier would rush over and spoil it. All the while sneering at the deceived prisoner. Why all this cruelty, you might ask. One explanation was that the camp was an isolated community without any conventional moral laws or ethical codes. Another was that the SS men had been raised in an authoritarian state and had to obey orders blindly. Above whom, there were men with great power and above them all, there was the Führer. He couldn't be held accountable for anything; he was equal to God since he had the power to extinguish life or let people live.

In an authoritarian state, everything is a matter of obeying orders. The subordinate had to rely on those in charge, the superior was always right. That was the law of camp-hierarchy. Some of them were sadists. But above all, there were loyal and dutiful soldiers who never asked any questions. Just like there were many good German citizens in the society who never asked any questions. It was the dutiful, the passives and the obedient ones who made the system and the Holocaust possible. Disobedience was severely punished. There were also other types of camps in Germany for those in opposition and the dissidents. Primarily, it was all about a foolish idea: people were divided into different races, and one race was assumed to be better than the others. An unacceptable assumption, one might think, in times characterized by humanity. But it was also about misuse of power. And taking advantage of our despair. Contempt for others, which in fact is self-contempt in disguise. The exploitation of cowardice. And of the misdirected obedience. Fascism arises in such a climate, even today.

CHAPTER 10

A DEATH MARCH FOR MY FATHER

The last winter of the war, 1945, was extremely cold. Heavy snow fell, and the cold crept into one's marrow. As long as you had the energy to keep moving, you were all right, but as soon as you stopped, you would be frozen. Many friends froze to death. It happened quickly. During a break I noticed that the prisoner next to me no longer responded. He had a peculiar gaze upon his face. When I touched him, he was ice cold. Sometimes there were civilians who supervised the work. They could show some compassion to us. This time we managed to convince the foreman to save a human's life by sharing his liquid ration. At the last moment, we pried open the frozen prisoner's mouth. We poured some hot liquid in him. Then he came back to life.

The cold made you slow and drowsy. One unusually cold winter day, I received a slap in the face from a command because I didn't respond to his order fast enough. Afterward I went about with lid for my ear. The pain increased gradually, and it felt as if my head was about to explode. One night I couldn't stand the pain any longer. In pure despair, I went out with the risk of being shot, and I let it all out by screaming loudly. Something burst. Warm blood and pus ran out of my ear. Later on I learned the scream saved my hearing.

During the winter, the front line came closer day by day. In the far distance, we could hear the bombers on their way to their assigned targets. The raids were primarily directed toward industries and mines located in strategically important Silesia but also toward Berlin, which was under heavy attacks during this last winter of war. We could hear the gunfire and even the gleam of the explosions caused by the bombings. And we could see the antiaircraft pieces in the air. Since we neither had radio nor newspaper, we didn't know who was shooting. Rumor had it the Allies were close by, and they were coming to liberate us. As early as 1944, it was clear for all, except for the Nazis, that Germany was about to lose the war. Bombs fell only a few kilometers from Auschwitz-Birkenau. Our hope grew stronger every day. Hope was the reason we survived.

In the early spring of 1945, as the Red Army was approaching the area where we were, the Nazi leaders ordered all camps to be evacuated. Two months before the end of war, the Nazis believed in victory, at least officially. Therefore, they moved the entire camps to more secure locations up-country. Perhaps they strongly believed we, slave workers, would help them build the new Reich, now that the old was falling apart and turned into ruins. Auschwitz-Birkenau was evacuated sooner than the work camps. The prisoners at the extermination camps were too weak to march the long distance toward Germany. They loaded the wagons with the sick and dying prisoners, set toward Bergen-Belsen, Buchenwald, and the other camps located on German ground.

Despite the exhaustion and the diseases, most of the prisoners in our camp were able-bodied, in the camp command's point of view. Some of the elderly, severely sick, and starving prisoners were excluded. My father was one of those who was counted as too weak to be able to march. According to rumors, they were supposed to be transported to Dernau. They would be executed upon arrival. Reality turned out to be otherwise. The prisoners who were left behind would be liberated long before us. Who knew what to foresee? I could visualize how Wolf would give the order to the execution squad and how the prisoners would sink down in the dirt at the shooting site. I had to save my father. As we were about to march off, at the very last moment and forcefully, I pulled my father into our group. The commandant didn't notice my move due to the present confusion. My father was reluctant. "Let me stay," he said.

"You have to come with me," I told him. "This is your only chance to be saved."

Imagine that—I was so wrong about what we were about to face. What was supposed to be his rescue became his downfall. The thought of it is still hurtful.

The march became a nightmare. No preparations whatsoever, except for some food for the soldiers.

Nobody told us where we were going. At the final stage of the war, there was total confusion. Several thousands of camp prisoners were moving forward in a seemingly infinite trail. We found ourselves in deserted agricultural regions with a few villages at a long distance from each other. Out in these fields, we were hardly seen. Those who could see us kept out of sight. The air raids continued around us and even intensified as bombs fell over cities and villages. We didn't care; we could barely react to the explosions. We had to keep on moving, purely mechanical, despite our sore feet and aching muscles. There was a serious risk of being shot, if you fell to the ground. We heard the shots continually during the entire march. A great many fell. The half-dead and the dead bodies were kicked aside, the march went on without interruption.

It was in the beginning of March and still cold. Since our own shoes had already fallen apart, most of us had wrapped pieces of fabric round our feet. Some used newspaper, which was better against the cold, but soon it was torn to shreds. No warm outer garments were handed out. We cowered whenever we could to keep warm. And we kept on marching. I held on to my father in a tight grip. He became weaker and weaker. Perhaps psychologically he reached the crossing line for what a human can bear. Something that happened just before his death, speaks for it. We passed by a village. There was a six-story-high factory building. Everywhere, out of every window, women were leaning out and shouting something in different languages that we didn't understand. My father lost it totally. "Margit! Margit!" My mother's name. "Edith! Elisabeth!" My elder sisters. His voice was broken. "Medi! Judith!" The youngest. He shouted out their names as loud as he could again and again. I tried to calm him down, but he resisted and wanted to break free so he could run inside the building. He was convinced that some of our relatives were in there. The women were overexcited too. Many of them tried to send down messages. Scraps of paper tied to cotton threads were tossed through the windows like confetti. Handwritten notes in several languages. "Is Jakob Klein alive?" "Has anybody seen Leo Rosenblum?" They were all looking for their relatives, and so were we. The German soldiers brutally drove us away from the factory building, which must have been some sort of a penalty camp or a collection point for women on the run. We could still hear their despairing cries, long after we had left the place. My father was inconsolable, so he just cried. He couldn't let go of the thought that my mother and my sisters were inside that building.

The march went on nonstop. An older German soldier marched right beside me. He carried a heavy load. Even though he was in a much better shape than I was, he had some trouble carrying the large backpack. When we stopped for a break, he lifted over his gasket on me. I thought I would receive some bread as a reward. I carried that heavy gasket for several hours; he didn't even say thank you when I handed it back to him. It became dark but we didn't stop to encamp. The march continued forward, mechanically. Most of us were in a state of trance. It was as if we both walked and slept at the same time. The next day, my father was completely exhausted. I was also exhausted, and I couldn't support him any longer. A large wagon was in the back of the trail. "Those who can't walk may get a lift," a German soldier offered. I was very suspicious and concerned. Why should the Germans suddenly care about us? This time my father was unyielding. He followed the soldier. I would never see him again. We passed through a larger village. The soldiers didn't want to scare ordinary people by executing prisoners in the middle of the streets. The weakest ones were gathered and transported to the nearest forest to be executed quietly. Those marching at the back of the trail saw the wagon turn toward the woods. Soon after we heard gunshots. My father died, even though I refused to accept it there and then.

The march went on, and the pace was insane. The soldiers were constantly ready to shoot. Those who stumbled or fell were shot right at the spot. Nothing could slow us down. A man in front of me slightly wobbled. The soldier walking right beside him shot him in the head. He wore a warm fur hat; it fell right before my feet. Since I didn't have a hat, and I was cold, I grabbed the fur hat with a bullet hole, brain matter, and blood. I put it on my head without stopping for a single moment. I could have been shot too.

It was impossible to continue without a break. Finally, we camped on a field near a small lake. Well, it was not a real camp exactly, because we had to lie down on the ground with our jackets as the only protection against the cold. There was a rumor among the prisoners that the German soldiers had orders to shoot us in our sleep since we were too many and too slow to walk. That night, many of us didn't dare to sleep. But we saw another sunrise and the light warmed our stiff and frozen bodies. It was spring and the grass had just grown a bit. We were all starving so some came up with a brilliant idea to make fire and cook some soup with the fresh grass. Soon, that beautiful green grassy field was turned into a ruin. All vegetation was gone. All that was left was the bare earth. Everyone grabbed as much grass as they could and chewed it like herds of animals. Also, the buds and conifers on the trees were plucked. Afterward, it looked like as if the place had been visited by a swarm of harmful insects.

I was lucky enough to find a piece of bone buried in the ground. All the meat was gone, and the bone was dirty, but there was some gristle left to nibble on. I got in the line in order to heat up the bone in the fire. *At least it would get clean*, I thought. It started to sizzle and ooze. The hunger was excruciating so I couldn't wait for the bone to cool down. With a voracious appetite, I started to chew the bone. It burned my mouth and I felt the heat and the sharp edges of the bone as it passed through my gullet. It would take a long time before I was able to eat and drink without any pain. Yet another day of marching passed, and many died. The soldiers pushed us forward, but they become more and more tired and agitated. The road was paved by dead bodies. Those of us who had some energy left continued to march, mechanically as before. I was oddly numbed. My father was gone, I missed him so much. Yet I couldn't grasp the whole truth. That he was dead. I felt terribly abandoned.

On the third day we reached a railroad. Here we were supposed to be loaded onboard railway wagons. We still didn't know anything about our destination. This was just two months before the war ended. Strangely enough, even during this very last desperate march toward the disintegrating German Reich, it seemed as if they still believed in victory. Incredible superweapons that nobody had heard of or seen would make Germany invincible. But in fact the days of the Reich were numbered.

CHAPTER 11

LIBERATED BY THE RUSSIANS

The journey would take us to Buchenwald, outside Weimar. It was one of the most notorious camps, known in the Nazi Germany as a concentration camp for the opponents of the government. The camp had a capacity for more than eighty thousand prisoners. When the Allied forces arrived in April 1945, there were only twenty thousand prisoners still alive.

The wagon was more crowded than ever before. We were probably about eighty people in the wagon I was pushed into. Here there was no room for a latrine bucket, even less a place to sit. The most afflicted ones screamed in pain and panic. The screams eventually fell silent. The throbbing sound of the railway joints cradled everyone in a sleep-like condition, whilst the severely sick ones lost consciousness. They remained leaning over those who still had some strength left. Many died during our journey to Buchenwald, although they were holding on to the living as if in a dance-macabre, a medieval death dance. Those who sank down to the floor, were trampled down, if they were still alive, they would be trampled to death by the other prisoners.

The train stopped only once. The doors suddenly opened. Unaccustomed as we were to the light, we were not able to see what was about to happen. A food-ration was handed out. The soldiers threw the bread inside the wagons. All the prisoners tried to reach for a piece of bread, pulling at each other's clothes and fighting to access some bread. Many prisoners were squeezed to death. Needless to say, the soldiers could have handed out the bread in a more dignified way. It was rather the rule than the exception that prisoners were injured during transportations. All means of killing the prisoners were allowed.

Upon arrival to Buchenwald, we were ordered to carry the dead bodies out of the wagons. Faster! Faster! We were too slow, as usual. The SS men started to beat up those who stood nearby with their whips and rifle-butts, completely without distinction. I received a massive blow to my head and blood ran all over my face. Strange though, I didn't feel any pain. That thick fur hat soothed the blow somehow. And it was stuck in the wound, which soon became badly infected. The coagulated blood with the fur turned into a pie. I was no longer able to take it off, which, of course, worsened the infection.

I ended up in the same barrack as a couple of hundred other prisoners. They were all only fragments of humans left in silence, in apathy, befuddled by hunger and pain. Some had swollen up, so they were unrecognizable. Others had been transformed into the living dead who had already given up hope and lost their will to live. The only human feature on the living dead was their eyes. Back in Auschwitz, these prisoners were usually picked out for execution. In Buchenwald, they didn't even care to shoot them, they were left to die whatever the way. This was the waiting room of death. Dead bodies were everywhere, in the shower rooms and by the latrine buckets. Many of those still alive were blind.

Empty and sore eye-sockets were common. The guards preferably aimed for the head, perhaps to extinguish the eerie gaze of the living dead. Many could no longer stand up or walk.

There wasn't much left of what once was called the camp routine. We all had to go to the assembly area, regardless of what condition we were in. Those of us who had some strength left, had to carry the others and make sure they stood upright until the assembly was over. Those who couldn't stand on their feet and fell down remained on the ground. The guards and SS no longer seemed to care about the strict military discipline, even though they retained unrestricted power over us. Here not only did we have to look out for SS but also the two sadists who were in charge of our block as elders. At nights, when we were lying in our bunks, they amused themselves on our behalf. They played games such as "Who can strike down a prisoner in the shortest possible time?" They made bets and kept records of their victories and bragged about their achievements. They enjoyed the power they had over us and they could do anything they wanted with it.

By this time, in the middle of April, there was a total state of dissolution in the formerly well-organized Third Reich. The Allied forces had crossed over Rhine, at Remagen, the only bridge that remained unharmed, due to a misunderstanding. Therefore, they accomplished something that nobody had ever done before. The Allies had taken the German fortress and walked over the bridge. During April, the battles went on far inside the country. Approaching from three different front lines in the west, the Allies were heading for Berlin. In the East, the Red Army had reached Berlin suburbs. Bomb raid after bomb raid devastated the historical German cities and turned them into ruins. Many civilians perished.

According to Hitler's tactics and direct orders, nothing was supposed to end up in the hands of the conquerors. So the German army burned and destroyed everything in their path. Everywhere in the big cities and the villages people were starving. There were homeless, hopeless deserters, and refugees everywhere. There was complete chaos.

Order came that some parts of Buchenwald were to be evacuated. As we were boarding the trains, some of us were unable to stand up, those prisoners were cast inside like rag dolls. I was able to stand on my own feet. The train continued eastward. We passed by the front line and further into no-man's-land. We crossed the border to Czechoslovakia. When we finally reached our destination and the train stopped, we were safe. The German troops had moved toward the battle lines further in Germany and the Russian troops had not yet reached our location. Formally, it was still war, and we were still prisoners.

Where the train stopped was the end of the line. There was a factory on the side with a loading platform. I leaped out of the wagon and fell on the concrete, totally exhausted. All the prisoners were cast down on the loading platform, and we remained there, dead and alive alike. A group of curious people started to gather around us, the newcomers. They were prisoners, too, but in much better shape than we. They stared at us, in marvel and fright. Some of the bravest ones threw some bread and sugar lumps toward us. One lump of sugar fell within reach. I had never tasted anything that good.

We had come to Theresienstadt, previously known as a flagship camp. It was located six miles to the north from Prague. In the beginning of the war, some official representatives from international aid organizations, such as the Red Cross, had visited the camp to inspect and make sure that laws were in order, and the prisoners were well treated. As the camp orchestra played, the guests walked around in the seemingly pleasant urban-like facility with well-arranged gardens and meticulously renovated buildings from the turn of the century. They didn't suspect the evil in progress. Everywhere they looked there were fully vital prisoners busy doing some easy work, and they all assured the Red Cross there was nothing to complain about. Theresienstadt was a backcloth. Behind that well-directed act there was the exact same horrendous power at work as in Auschwitz and all the other concentration camps.

But now the SS had no power or control over the camp. Here we would be treated well. I received immediate care. I weighed only thirty-four kilos. My normal weight was twice as much. I was unable to walk. Instead, I crawled like a baby. The doctor was a prisoner too. He had worked at the camp for many years. He was a wise and gentle man who managed to do much with small means. I had a severe infection in one finger, since I had helped a soldier to mop the floor and accidentally cut my finger on a rusty nail. It seemed my finger had to be amputated. Another infection was about to work its way into my head, where the fur hat was stuck in the coagulated blood due to the punch I had received from the SS officer. Perhaps you might think that an amputated finger sounds like a triviality compared to the conditions I have described here. But to me it meant the definite end of my dream to become a pianist. "Save the finger," I begged the doctor. He understood and most likely did his best to help me, despite the limited and primitive instruments available to him. He knew this was probably my chance to survive, that the hope of a better future and a decent life was somehow attached to the fate of my finger. The old doctor saved my finger and managed to cut away the fur hat from my head. It was filled with solidified blood and dirt. Thanks to sufficient food rations and proper healthcare, I was able to walk again after a few weeks. I was recovering relatively fast, but I was still in need of care. I was restless. I wanted to move on.

On May 8, 1945, we were liberated by the Russians. The whole area became Russian occupation zone, awaiting the final peace order. When the Russian soldiers arrived, they were greeted as liberators. I remember I went out to the streets to join the celebration, although I still felt weak and fatigued. A long military vehicle cortege passed by the streets. People stood in clusters around the road. A Russian tank made a halt right in front of me. All of a sudden, I had an idea. "May I join you?" I asked in faltering Russian.

"Jump in," the Russian soldiers replied. They were all about the same age as I was. Suddenly I found myself under Russian protection without any belongings, with no money, quite carefree, with my legs dangling from a lorry behind the Russian tank. Finally, I was on my way home. Home. To Velký Sevluš. Maybe I would meet my mother or one of my sisters there. With that hope in sight, I started a long and arduous journey that offered many unexpected turning points. I had chosen to live on.

CHAPTER 12

I WAS A SKELETON WITH LIVE EYES

My whim to leave Theresienstadt saved my life. A few days after I left the camp, a typhus epidemy broke out. Many died before the help reached them. The entire Czech countryside seemed to be in movement. Minor battles went on here and there.

There were still a few days left until the Germans surrendered. Out in the countryside, the soldiers had totally lost all contact with the battle command. Some units kept defending themselves furiously against the giant Russian superpower. But most of them gave up without a fight. German soldiers were returning home and you could find them everywhere in small, disorganized groups. They were exhausted and hungry, but it seemed that many of them were relieved that the war was over. At this point the invincible Wehrmacht made such a miserable impression. A Russian tank evoked respect. Russian soldiers were dreaded for their cruelty in battle. German soldiers came walking alongside the road. As soon as they saw us, they dropped their weapons and raised their arms up high as a sign of surrender. The Russians continued toward Prague and didn't care about the Germans at all. They had their orders.

I hadn't been able to eat properly for more than a year. I had trouble keeping the food because I suffered from the chronic camp-diarrhea. Yet I was constantly, ravenously hungry. The Russians gave me plenty of food. They cut large slices of their dark, grain bread and carved out pieces of the heavily smoked and fatty ham, which was their own daily provision. I gobbled up everything they gave me. A short while later, I would feel the abdominal cramping. A starving man must get used to eating again gradually and carefully, but none of us knew that.

In the city called Mesice, about two miles from Prague, there were ongoing battles. At this point I was an unnecessary ballast. The Russian soldiers left me, like a cabbage at the city square. Since I had horrible stomachache and nausea, I remained there lying on the cobblestones, wailing with pain. Presumably, I suffered from colic. After a while, I managed to stand up on my feet and dragged myself to a little church. Right by the entrance to the church, there was a bench fixed to the wall where I laid down to rest for a while. I must have fallen asleep. When I woke up, I heard voices. There was a trial going on inside the church. A hearing was held with a Czech collaborator, a man who had cooperated with the Germans and betrayed his countrymen. Ordinary people wanted to administer justice without any official involvement. The man was sentenced to death. I heard footsteps approaching and I pretended to be asleep as I was afraid and felt terribly ill. If they noticed that I had been eavesdropping, I would be in big trouble, I figured. Squealers were everywhere. A man came over and shook me. I am on my way home, I tried to explain in Czech. The man stared at me with a blank look. Camp prisoner, I whispered. Liberated in Theresienstadt. He understood that.

By this time, the news about what had happened at the concentration camps, started to spread. Maybe it wasn't so strange that the man immediately believed me. I hardly looked human, more like an oddly human-looking ape, dressed in ridiculously oversized and badly fitting clothes.

My stomachache became worse. The man saw what a terrible state I was in. Carefully, he helped me to stand up and took me home. His mother received me. She didn't care that I was lousy, smelled badly and probably had infectious diseases. They took off my clothes and laid me down in a bed with clean and fragrant sheets.

My condition started to deteriorate and became critical. The man understood that he had to act quickly. All of a sudden, I found myself in a Russian military jeep. Driving on bumpy little roads that would take me to a castle, which had been converted into a provisional hospital. A nurse came out and lifted me up as if I was a little child. It was a remarkable contrast, coming to such a different environment. The baroque halls, the gold-framed mirrors from the floor to the ceiling, made the castle to look more like a dream. A care worker took off my clothes and carried me to the bathroom. We happened to pass by one of those large mirrors. For the first time in a year, I caught a glimpse of someone whose appearance scared me. It was my face, my body but everything was tremendously changed. What I saw now was a skeleton with live eyes. I never forget that sight.

I still had the weight of a ten-year-old child, the same as in Theresienstadt. Here at the castle, I received all the help I needed, and they could offer. Yet I didn't really feel sick, more fatigued. The worst affliction was hunger. I ate continually, day and night.

The nights were agonizing; I could never sleep. During those three weeks, I gained more than twenty kilos, which caused huge problems in my stomach and digestion. I was obsessed with food. My mind was constantly occupied with thoughts of food and the risk that it could be taken away from me. Like an animal, I hid pieces of bread and sausage everywhere. And I ate when no one was watching.

There was plenty of food at the castle, but not enough medication. It was also difficult for them to make a diagnosis. I was to be observed for further examination. It took a while. I was impatient and wanted to leave. The rumor that a camp prisoner was at the castle, spread quickly in the neighborhood. Unexpectedly, two boys came to visit me. Without telling me anything, they kindly asked me to go with them. I was utterly bored, the boys seemed to be my age and I was curious. Thy assisted me out to a waiting car. We drove off. The boys were members of a resistance movement against Nazism. They were sturdy and tough, used to being in charge of death and life. In a nearby barn, there were three SS officers who had been captured by the resistance. We found them in the straw, pinioned at different poles. They were imprisoned, pending trial, very likely similar to the one I unintendedly witnessed at the church. The young partisans interpreted justice in their own way. Therefore, they wanted to grant me a chance to take revenge. I felt sick. One of them came crawling toward me, the others seemed to be listless and just watched the whole thing. The man was terrified. He cried and begged. He did everything he could to be pardoned. One of the boys put a gun in my hands. "Now it's your turn," he said. But I didn't want to kill. I was fed up with death. Disgusted, I turned the other way. I didn't want to become a murderer. An executioner like the men who lay there and begged for their lives. None like those who boldly mistreated and humiliated scared prisoners. None like those who jeered on and obviously took pleasure in letting their whips whine.

There is always a choice in life. I couldn't even hate the SS men there, as they were crawling around, begging for their lives. I choose to believe that my upbringing and the love I had received as a child, made a crucial significance at this moment. I handed over the gun to one of the young partisans and asked to leave. There are lines, one should never cross.

Four weeks passed. Staying for such a long time at the hospital was just too much for me. Being restless as I was, I didn't give myself enough time to be fully examined. I kept thinking about Velký Sevluš, my mother and my sisters. Perhaps I was still hopeful my father would be alive. I didn't want to realize that he had been executed. The hospital was located about two miles from Prague. Prague, like most other cities in Central Europe, had become a center for all those who were searching for their relatives, I figured. I hoped that I would at least, meet my fellow countrymen.

Prague wasn't so damaged by the war, but the city was occupied. There were Russian soldiers everywhere. In other words, it was quite dangerous to stay in Prague and I was soon to be aware of that. A decent farmer gave me a lift on his horse carriage. So I came to Prague with high expectations, totally unaware of the current situation. The Russian soldiers were looking for suspects in every corner and street, which basically meant anybody without a valid passport or identification. You could of course purchase such documents on the black market, but people like me with no money were lawless. The Russian soldiers caught everyone who drifted about with no lodging. Frightened and frozen people tried to hide here and there.

Without proper identification, you could be deported to Russian work camps, to Siberia at worst.

I didn't even know which nationality I belonged to. Preferably, I would like to be considered as Czech. Which embassy could I turn to? Nevertheless, it was impossible for me to prove my identity since I had lost everything. We were many Hungarians in the same desperate situation. Needless to say, I was caught and together with other refugees, state- and homeless, as well as a group of Czech drifters, were directed down to a cellar. I had survived so many hazards, so I had no plans to let myself be captured by the Russians and transported further to a work camp. *There must be a way out*, I thought. I was used to find my way in the darkness. In a secluded corner, I managed to find a high-positioned-window. By stacking some broken chairs, I could build something to climb on. We were about forty prisoners who escaped this way. Then I realized that Prague wasn't a safe place for someone with no secure identity or money and uncertain descent. I was impatient, worried and longed for my home. I had to move on.

CHAPTER 13

BACK HOME

I had sixty miles before me. It would have been a long journey even under normal circumstances. Now the country was shattered by the war. The railway and bus connections were awful. The roads had been partially bombed. I had to walk long distances on foot. After walking for about half a kilometer, I had to stop and rest. My feet hurt with every step I took. I carried a disease of which I knew nothing yet. But I had no energy and felt weak.

If I were lucky, I would be able to get a ride on a horse carriage. The farmers didn't mind helping someone in need of assistance. Since my identification papers were not in order, I did my best to avoid big cities. My experience in Prague had scarred me for life. In smaller cities and villages in rural areas, I was protected as I could easily blend in like any other ranging peasant. The clothes I received in Theresienstadt, didn't capture any attention. People were used to not being well-dressed in the countryside. I knocked on doors and begged for food, which usually worked just fine. There was a willingness to help, in the wake of the war. But finding lodging was more difficult. Apparently, I made a weird impression. I was unnaturally thin, uncut and unshaven with a disheveled appearance. Nobody dared to let me in their home. It was May and the nights were still cold, since I had no money, I had to sleep outside. I tried to keep warm by covering myself with newspapers.

There were no highways leading to Velký Sevluš. To find my way home on tiny, winding country roads wasn't an easy task under any circumstances. I didn't have a map, so I tried to find the way by asking the farmers, who gave me a lift. Somebody pointed in one direction. Somebody else pointed in another direction. I took a southern route. Unintentionally, I would end up in a small town in Rumania. I had generally avoided people in the countryside, unless I had to ask for help. In Satu Mare, a town near the Czech border, I met several Jews who had survived the Holocaust. Some of them lived there, and they had come back to their homes. Others were lost, drifting about, searching for their relatives like me. At the small town square, I suddenly saw a man sitting on a park bench in the sun, conversing with a group of people. Meeting him was totally unexpected, almost as a shock.

The man in front of me wasn't supposed to be alive. I used to call him Uncle Braun. He was about the same age as my father, and he was a fellow prisoner at the last work camp. What hurt the most was my very last memory of him that was etched firmly on my mind. The picture was crystal clear. Uncle Braun stood together with my father among those who had been discarded right before the long march. His face was all swollen, his legs and feet were as thick as elephant legs. I saw him being lifted up on the back of a truck since he was too weak to crawl up by himself. He was supposed to be transported to Dernau to be executed. He was standing right in front of me now, like a ghost. I couldn't wait any longer; I had to know. "What happened to the others from the camp?" I asked.

"Shortly after arrival to the camp, the Russians attacked," Uncle Braun told me.

The German soldiers fled, so they didn't have the time to shoot the prisoners. Otherwise, that was usually the case because the Germans did their best to get rid of unwanted witnesses. The day after, the prisoners were liberated by the Red Army. I remembered how persistent I had been, forcing my father to go with me. Was it my fault he wasn't here standing right beside Uncle Braun? I was desperate to hear an answer, but Braun just looked at me in silence. Obviously, he had no answers.

There are truths that are too heavy to handle. Meeting uncle Braun was such a reminder to me. What I had done to my father was wrong. I had forced him to leave, to go with me on that long march. I couldn't change that now. The thought of the consequence of my actions, leading to my father's death was unbearable. And I had to live with that for the rest of my life. I began to feel an intense discomfort and I wished this reunion with Braun had never taken place. Without money and passport, I didn't stand a chance to make it. In Satu-Mare, I had the opportunity to obtain a temporary identification if someone could confirm my identity. The only person there who knew me, was Braun. Together we went to the police. "I have been robbed," I said, though it wasn't true.

Uncle Braun nodded in agreement. "The boy is telling the truth. He is OK."

I received my identity documents. Now, I was able to move freely and didn't have to be afraid of getting arrested all the time. The other Jews in Satu-Mare told me that more help was offered to those in need, in Bucharest, the capital of Rumania. There were many American aid organizations working there to help survivors. Bucharest had become a center for one of many Jewish

American organizations that tried to help their supporters in Europe. There was also the Red Cross to convey inquiries and sometimes they could pass on information about the missing people. In Bucharest, there was one of the few operative American embassies in Central-Europe. The diplomatic relations between the United States and Hungary were breached in 1942. After that, it was dangerous to possess American documents. My mother burned everything that could prove we were American citizens. But we memorized grandfather's address carefully. Perhaps I could contact him through the embassy in Bucharest.

Velký Sevluš or Bucharest? Perhaps I was afraid to be confronted with more unpleasant truths and a reality I surmised but couldn't accept. Perhaps I was simply afraid of returning home. I decided to sort things out before heading back home. So I was back on the same ragged and shabby roads that brought me through Czechoslovakia. Now I was on my way to Bucharest through Rumania. After spending so many weeks on the countryside, I thought the decayed city of Bucharest felt like the big world. I watched the well-dressed city dwellers, the houses, and the cafés with wide-open eyes. I was as hungry for people and city life as I was for bread.

At the American embassy, I was received with a sense of blasé courtesy. My case was one among many, we were all looking for our relatives and none of us had any money. A clerk, who had probably heard the same story over and over again, sat with his feet on the desk and told me to come back in a week. I went to the American aid organization. They gave me money, proper identity documents and instruction on how to find a hotel room. And a change of clean clothes. Suddenly I was somebody, a person and no longer a number. That euphoria—joy is scarcely the right word—cannot be described. Like a rebirth. At the hotel,

I took a shower and put on the clean clothes. For the first time in more than a year, I was able to sleep alone, in a tidy room and in my own bed. In the middle of the night, I woke up by a familiar sting. Lice. I found two lice in the sheets. I started to cry. It felt like a relapse into dirt, disease, and distress. *Will this ever end?* I asked myself desperately.

Eventually, I received news about my grandfather through the embassy. I found out he had passed away only a few weeks after the war ended. There was no other news about my relatives. I had no reason to linger in Bucharest. From here, there was a direct train service toward Velký Sevluš. The American aid organization had indeed provided me with money. Nonetheless, I had to be frugal. Who knew when and how I was going to receive more? I hopped on a train with open luggage vans. I met other free riders in the same wagon. Immediately, I recognized two of them, they were sisters. Their hometown was very close to Velký Sevluš. I had visited that town several times since one of my uncles lived there. We just sat there in silence, quite shy and feeling awkward. Yet I felt such a joy to meet someone who I knew from the past.

The journey onboard the train was too slow. Finally, I saw the familiar train station. Outwardly, everything appeared to be the same. The war had spared Velký Sevluš. At the same time, I felt as if everything was somewhat peculiar. Something had changed and I felt such unexplainable anxiety. I had looked forward to this moment for a very long time. Something was wrong. The streets that were vibrant and alive before, seemed deserted and empty. The vivacious marketplaces were also completely empty due to the lack of food. I only saw a few passers-by who I recognized. The town had changed. This was no longer my hometown. I didn't feel welcome here. The people I met on the streets either avoided me or looked away. Perhaps I didn't want to catch people's eyes. I realized that I too had changed a lot. Not only my appearance.

My anxiety grew stronger. I walked faster, almost leaping forward with my heart pounding hard and iron taste in my mouth. There were only about five hundred meters from the train station to my home. But I was in a bad shape and with sweat running down my neck, I arrived in our street. Finally, I saw our house and I tried to calm myself down by walking slowly. Almost as if my mother would see me, calm and balanced although I was weak and worn out. I opened the gate to the little forecourt in front of the terraced houses. A neighbor stepped out of his door. He was very tall and looked down on me in surprise. That wasn't a friendly look. As if it wanted to say, "So you came back after all, Jew bastard!"

Our house seemed abandoned, although outwardly, it looked the same as usual. The windows were still barred, the door was nailed-up, as when the gendarmes took us away. It was right in that moment I suddenly understood the horrible truth: Nobody was there. Not my mother. Not my sisters. And I had to accept the fact I would never see my father alive again. The picture of the happy family reunion in our home, my mother welcoming me on the stairs, vanished like a dream upon awakening. Deep down, perhaps I knew it was nothing but a delusion. All that was left was sorrow and a sense of abandonment. My home was no longer my home, it was as strange as the town itself. I didn't even dare to loosen the planks used to seal the door. But I did have a peak through the slots, and I could see the house had been plundered. None of our personal belongings and furniture remained there. Without a single thought in my mind, I started walking the streets back to the station. What had happened was obvious. I couldn't deny the truth anymore. Panic, as well as a feeling of powerlessness, took over me. I couldn't think clearly anymore so I started running toward the station.

A train was just about to depart and I hopped onboard in the very last moment. I didn't care where it was heading to. Later, I was informed that out of those three thousand Jews who were deported, only a few had survived. In Velký Sevluš, it wasn't considered a disaster. On the contrary, the anti-Semitism was still alive, as strong as before. But I didn't think about that then, as the train was leaving. No thoughts about the future or what I was supposed to do. Despair grew into a vacuum in my inner being. I had but one thought. Away from Velký Sevluš.

CHAPTER 14

MY JOURNEY BEGINS

The train took me to Budapest. There I hoped to find my uncle and his family. What I mostly longed for, was the safety, only a family could provide. My nights were filled with nightmares. Ever since I left the camp, I was haunted by the images of dead bodies in decay. I could see their faces, their twisted limbs. It was the ever-growing pile of corpses outside the gate at Dernau that recurred over and over again. Sometimes I ran out in the middle of the night just to see a normal human face. I rarely took off my clothes when I went to bed. I lay down with all my clothes and shoes on, constantly ready to flee. I managed to sleep for a short while, until I woke up from the restless sleep with my heart pounding and a terrible nausea. Always the same nightmare, the distorted dead. In the dark, there was no escape from those fearful sights. Therefore, I often tried to sleep when it was light.

I had had a second home at my uncle's place in Budapest. It was with great anticipation and fear that I stepped out of the train at the partly burnt out and badly scarred train station. How different had it not been the last time I was there. There was nothing left of the elegant city from 1943 with its cheerful and blithe street life. The boulevards and Corson were crowded with scary and intimidating Russian soldiers. There was no sign of the Arrow Cross anymore. Those who had not been arrested or lynched, had withdrawn to anonymity. Instead, the streets were dominated by Russian soldiers in scruffy uniforms.

Budapest had paid the price for its liberation from the Nazis, at a very high cost. The final battle for Budapest took place around Christmas 1944. The Russians occupied Pest, the eastern part of the city. The Germans fled to Buda. There the German forces were held captive through a Russian pincer movement. Buda was the nice part of the city. Here there were the old imperial palace, diplomatic districts, among them the Swedish Legation where Raoul Wallenberg was active in the struggle to save Jews from Eichmann's deportations. And also, the rich men's private castles as well as the opera and the music conservatory and all the other historical monuments. Everything would be destroyed.

The Buda side was exposed to massive fire by the Russians through air raids and Stalin organs—that is, the notorious Russian rocket launchers that effectively crushed the German defense lines. There was hardly one single house that remained undamaged under the Russian fire. The Red Army was infamous for its brutality. Liberation was mostly a massacre. Russian soldiers intoxicated with vodka shot at civilian people for no reason. They raped women who had greeted them with open arms. Soldiers went up and down the streets with flamethrowers and burned down houses to wipe out fascists, as they called it. But in fact, it was just a matter of meaningless destruction. People were either burned inside or badly hurt.

When the Germans surrendered, the looting started. Carloads of carpets, furniture and watches went straight to Soviet. The Russians were particularly interested in wristwatches. I have no idea why this fixation. Soldiers boasted in wearing up to ten watches on each arm to show off. I tell you this, to show you the true face of the war. Budapest was violated. The historical bridges that the Germans had blown up as they escaped from Pest, were replaced with small ferries and temporary bridges. One of them was adorned with a grotesque portrait of Stalin.

As soon as I got off the train and stepped out into the street bustle, I came across "Ivan," the sobriquet of the Russian soldiers. They walked about in squads of ten, with heavy-loaded weapons hanging by the belt. They were supposed to monitor the general order, but they used their power to harass ordinary people. Everywhere in the streets and round the corners, there were dead bodies. The killing was ongoing especially in public places and in daylight so that it would draw attention.

The dead often lay there for days—nobody dared or could bury them. Sometimes they were covered with newsprint. The Nazi terror had turned into a new one. One way to harass the people of Budapest was to stop everyone and to ask for identity documents. Documents! They shouted at all who passed by.

Since many of them were illiterate, almost anything could suffice as identification paper, even bread coupons—a trick that I tried myself. If you were not fast enough to present your document or for some reason managed to annoy Ivan, you would be called a spy. Their method of conduct was done in a foul manner. They would show how to cut out a person's eyes by using the little finger and forefinger. Or they just shot someone without a warning. Sometimes they would stab the victims with a knife.

Destruction and terror were all I saw on my way to Orczi Utca 38, the street where my relatives lived. Or at least had lived, I hardly dared to think otherwise. The street was located a bit from the center. Their neighborhood seemed to be relatively well. The housing shortage was huge due to the fact so many people had lost their homes. An allocation authority had seized abandoned properties, split up those that were considered to be too big for a family and distributed them among the homeless. The distribution was totally random.

When I knocked on the door at my uncle's house, a stranger opened. Two families had been allocated there temporarily. My aunt Iren had moved into the smallest room of the apartment, the maid's chamber. Rest of that spacious five-room apartment had been distributed. The previous comfort of my uncle's well-kept residence was gone. Instead, there was only disorder.

I embraced Iren and I held her tight for a long time. Where are the others? I asked. She told me that the family was scattered, not long after I returned to Sevluš. One afternoon, my uncle Bumi and my cousin Erzsi had gone out for a walk. It turned out to be a huge mistake, because they never came back. This was during the terror of Arrow Cross. It was uncertain if they were still alive. But my aunt refused to believe that they were dead. Every day, she waited and expected their return. In her tiny room, she had squeezed in Erzsi's grand piano and a small place for her to sleep. Gabor, the boy, was safe though.

I realized that I could not stay there. So I went out and wandered about without knowing what to do. By chance, I came across a Jewish organization. Many young drifters gathered in Budapest. A lot of them were Jews, almost with the same background as I. There were also some illegal Jewish organizations. The leaders were Zionists, but we who sought them, were generally quite uninterested in politics. What we all had in common was the fact we were alone, homeless, and we searched for our relatives. Next year in Jerusalem! That was the traditional greeting during the great Easter meal for the Jews. To most of us, it was just something we said to each other, like a phrase. But historically, the dream of Israel as an independent Jewish state, had been with us for two thousand years. By the end of the 1800s, there was a political movement whose goal was to establish Israel on the land that, according to Jewish tradition, was given to the Jews by God.

After the war, due to our situation, the dream of having our own country grew ever stronger. We wanted to settle down in Israel, in order to avoid the sense of rootlessness we all had. And to be able to diminish our longing after the dear ones we had lost, by starting a new community. A dream of starting a new life among our fellow believers so that we could be safe from anti-Semitism. Although we learned that anti-Semitism was not exactly erased as the crimes of Nazism were revealed. Perhaps the sense of belonging to a certain fellowship, was the strongest reason why I joined the Zionist organization. Obviously, Israel was attractive as well. And I wanted to get away, far away from the Europe that treated us as "Jewish-bastards" and "scum".

Through the secret organization, I was offered a place at a collective. Most of the people living there, were about my age, between twenty and twenty-five years old of both genders. The collective was forced to exist illegally. There was a serious conflict between the communists and the Zionists, which at times was quite fierce. If you had any collaboration with Jewish groups, you were considered to be a traitor or a spy, in the eyes of the Russians. And if you, in addition to that, didn't have your papers in order then you would be in serious trouble. Personally, I had only those temporary documents I received in Bucharest, nothing officially Hungarian. The other members of the Jewish organization were in the same situation.

Therefore, we lived together in the greatest possible secrecy. Our accommodation was temporary too, we could be asked to move someplace else or evicted at any moment. I was the only one in the group who was fluent in Russian. That's why I had a special role in the group. A former Russian Jewish officer joined us. He gave me his old uniform jacket. Together with a pair of khaki trousers I let sew and a pair of leather boots, I looked like a real Russian officer. At least, if you didn't look too carefully. The uniform jacket made me look rather cool and bold. At first I carried it over my arm, trying not to draw so much attention to myself in case I didn't behave like a Russian. But soon enough I was wearing it all the time.

To play a Russian soldier was dangerous. But the suspense of it was tempting. It felt like a compensation for the year I had lost in captivity. I was now the master of the situation. It was worth the price, even though, I lived in constant fear. One night, I had the greatest benefit of the uniform scam. One evening in September, I was visiting my aunt and I decided to stay the night as it was getting late. I received a phone call in the middle of the night. Come here immediately, a voice said. It was one of my friends at the collective. Russian soldiers are here. I threw on my jacket, the khaki trousers and the boots. And I did my best to look strictly like a proper officer, despite the urgency. The tramway halls were located very close by. All traffic had stopped because it was very late. I could have caught a taxi, but there were no cars in suburban areas. *How was I supposed to get out of there*? I thought.

The light was on inside the halls, so I had an idea. There must be someone inside. I managed to find a bell and there was a half-asleep night-guard who came to the door. I gave the guard an order to make a tram available at once. Actually, I didn't know how I could convince him, but I spoke in Hungarian with a fake Russian accent. I must have appeared quite friendly with authority. Probably he was surprised to see a well-behaved Russian officer; therefore he obeyed my order. Or he didn't dare to disobey. He disconnected a tram and put the track in order while he was swearing and muttering.

The collective was situated a few kilometers away but not exactly along any regular tram line. At every other block, the driver had to get out to change gears so that we could stay on the right track. He seemed more and more agitated every time he had to make a halt. Finally, we arrived at the right address. The soldiers had followed a girl. It was all about a clumsy hookup and they had no suspicions about us being spies or criminal elements. They simply didn't know where they were, but the situation was serious. The girl and the others in the group knew that I was on my way. They did their best to keep the soldiers in a good mood.

The Russian army had an extreme hierarchy. An officer only had to look upon a soldier to make him obey orders, I had heard. That would prove to be just right. The soldiers knew they had committed a crime against the military discipline as soon as they saw me entering the room. They quickly jumped to their feet and stood up in attention. I gave them a signal to leave, and they took off. We were safe, with sheer horror. But what would happen next time? It was time for us to break up. First I had to help my aunt to find Gabor and bring him home. She had not dared to go outside Budapest. It wasn't easy either to reach the countryside. Many refugees were out and about. The train connections were poorly. Boxcars, cattle-wagons, anything that could move was put into traffic. It could still not suffice. At all the stations, there were endless lines of people waiting. As soon as a train came in, it was immediately filled. At the risk of life, people traveled on the roofs and the footboards.

These terms didn't apply to the Russians though. For their sake, whole compartments had to be cleared out. When the Russians came in, the Hungarians had to move aside. I decided to travel in my uniform. Casually, I stepped in a train compartment. Everybody moved right away. In my well-practiced phony Hungarian accent, I asked them to stay. I saw some old and tired women who had to go out to the corridor together with some cranky children. I waved at them to come in. Don't trust the Russian, one of the old women said. But he has kind eyes, the other one replied.

A real Russian came wandering through the train to check on the passengers. As soon as he saw me from a distance, he turned around and disappeared. Presumably, he saw me as a superior officer and therefore left. Everybody in the compartment breathed out.

Gabor was staying at some Christian friends' place in the countryside. The area was quite isolated and not so far from a little town about twenty miles outside Budapest. Gabor wanted to leave right away but there was no train until the next day. The evening turned out to be rather an odd experience. They prepared a spiritualistic séance. I was invited too. Gabor's "stepfather" was apparently a famous psychic who could contact dead people's spirits. A group of people gathered around a table. There were about twenty-five of them, mostly farmers from the area. Only one candle lit up the room. They grabbed each other's hands and shortly after they were all in a dreamlike state of mind. It was completely quiet in the room. In the center of the room, the psychic was deep into trance. Suddenly he began to speak in a strange voice. He had made contact with a spirit.

Some of the other participants tried to make him contact their dead relatives or to ask for advice about the future. I sat in a corner, felt like an outsider and didn't ask any questions. All of a sudden, he turned around toward me. He didn't know anything about me, what had happened to me or my plans to emigrate to Israel. Or about the insecurity I felt inside. He looked at me seriously and said: you have a long journey ahead of you. You are going to suffer a great deal and endure much sorrow. Of those you are searching for, there are only a few to be found. It turned out to be a very accurate prediction.

CHAPTER 15

TO ITALY AND BACK AGAIN

One of the darkest and the least noticed parts in the history of anti-Semitism is what happened after the Second World War. The concentration camps were emptied. Hundreds of thousands of people left the camps, most of them were severely ill and homeless from Eastern Europe. Only a few countries received stateless Jews. Therefore, the thought of an independent state in Israel achieved great support. At this time, Palestine was a British protectorate. The British were strongly against Jewish immigration. The independent state of Israel would threaten their position of power in the region and interfere with the mutual understanding between the Arab countries and the British government. The Palestinians were a weak group politically, organized in clans, and they had basically accepted the British supremacy.

What mattered the most to the British was their economic interests such as free passage through Suez Canal and the control of the oil. A Jewish migration would disturb the balance of power. Consequently, the Brits opposed to what was referred to as "uncontrolled migration" of Jews. Despite the fact there was an agreement on legal migration, the so-called Balfour

Declaration from 1917, where the demand of an independent state highly emerged from Zionist direction. Before the war, one of my cousins had emigrated to Palestine. Some discerning Jews had already realized what Nazism would bring about. Some made sure to take refuge in Palestine, others moved to the States or neutral countries.

At the collective, we made the decision that the time was up for departure. Through the Hungarian countryside, we would cross the Austrian border and then move forward to a city called Graz, near the Yugoslav border. We left in secret. The Jewish organization arranged all the documents and provided us with money. Our plan was to travel to southern Italy via Yugoslavia, from there we would be able to get to Palestine on boats that illegally transported refugees. My entire luggage consisted of a blanket, a change of clothes, and some family photos I received from my aunt. The photos were particularly dear to me. We often walked by night to avoid an encounter with the Russian military patrols. Shorter distances, we traveled by train. The critical spot was the border. We managed to get by one night without being noticed by the border guards.

Graz was the connecting point for a number of organizations that all took care of the illegal migration. Behind them, there were several organizations and associations, mostly American, that supported the idea of an independent Jewish state. All escape routes were secret. If one route had been tested and proven to be safe, next group could take the same. The task of finding safe routes, belonged to the Central. Agents and corrupt collaborators were everywhere. We had to wait for confirmation in Graz, in order to receive information about the safe arrival of the previous group.

There were thirteen people waiting in my group. We waited but the group was not heard of. Three weeks passed and no news from them. The leadership decided that we were good to go. We were fully aware of the dangerous journey ahead of us. The Brits had set up internment camps in Cyprus for those who illegally traveled to Palestine. Many who tried to enter Palestinian/British territory, ended up in prison.

The first destination was Italy. The way ahead was through a railroad tunnel. Even if it was considered to be safe, we had to be mindful of the fact the trains could pass by any moment. It was quite a dreadful experience in that narrow tunnel. The British agents who were monitoring all borders were more dangerous than the fast-passing trains. According to our fake documents, we were home-travelling Greeks who had been liberated from concentration camps. Together we pretended to speak Greek when people were around, and we really enjoyed our "homemade" language. It was easy for me to switch identity, because of my dark hair and my brown eyes. I could be a Greek, a Yugoslav, or an Italian. It was fun to act like a Greek for a change. Since I was quite good at pretending, I must have seemed credible even as a Greek.

The railroad tunnel led us into Yugoslavia. Once there we met Yugoslav partisans—General Tito's tough soldiers—who were in charge of the passport control. Tito was considered a war hero, and he had also succeeded in uniting the small states of the northern Balkans into one country. It is the same country we have seen fallen apart, but t it was a young nation filled with enthusiasm. Yugoslavia won the war so there was a kind of victory euphoria, totally unlike what we had seen in the old and weary countries of the Central Europe. Probably that was the reason why the partisans greeted us so well. They accepted our story. Maybe it wasn't so strange, considering how we looked. They might even have felt sorry for us. Luckily, none of the soldiers could speak Greek, otherwise we would have been caught. They granted us passage through the country and gave us a lift down the road in their jeeps. Before we departed, they wished us good luck.

Strangely enough, they never asked about how we were planning to get to Greece. We were heading toward a completely different direction, to Italy. Our next target was Trieste, a city located close to the Italian border. On the long bridge leading to the city, I saw the sun rise over the ocean. The sun spread its red light over the calm sea, like a path you could have taken right into the light. This was probably the most beautiful view I had ever seen in my life. Almost like a sign that life must go on.

Arriving in Italy was really dangerous. The British controlled everything, even Guardia Civil, the hardline semi-military Italian police force. They knew that most of the refugee boats came from Italy. We had our orders, to never linger and never talk to strangers, even though they seemed friendly. We travelled by train to Udine, a city in northern Italy. Udine was a junction for all kinds of communications. From there you could travel to many different directions. Perhaps that was the main reason why the British monitored this city. At this point we were very tired. We all longed for a good-night's sleep, a shower, and clean clothes. There was a car outside the station with Red Cross emblem on it, and there was a group of men who stood around it, holding Red Cross banners. I immediately became suspicious. Why would Red Cross staff wait outside a train station for incoming trains? They had probably received a tip about our group, or they just searched randomly. It was quite easy for a trained eye to distinguish us as a group. The British and their agents kept watching for everything that would count as organized "trips".

"Come with us," the men said. "You look like you need some food and some place to sleep." I figured it sounded too good to be true. They were profusely nice to us. Nobody in the group would listen to me, nobody would believe this was a trap. Some stepped into their cars. They quickly drove away through the town and approached a giant castle-like building with a huge gate, which slowly opened up as the cars entered the courtyard outside the house. There were two guards in military uniforms, in front of the gate. It looked nothing like Red Cross, even the most credulous of people could see that and admit. I had just stepped out of the car and walked inside the five-meter-high wooden gate, when I heard someone shout in Yiddish, "Stop! This is a trap. This is a British territory." That person belonged to our contact group. They had been captured in Udine and held there for weeks of interrogation. My entire group was right behind me, with their small bags and all exhausted after our long journey. And we all had but one choice. To leave as quickly as possible. The enormous gate was about to be closed, heavily and slowly. We managed to leave the premises at the very last moment, before the gate was shut and the guards could stop us. Run! I shouted. Break up! We see each other later at the station. We scattered all over the town, into dark alleys and gloomy streets. Later on, we gathered at dusk, found a freight train, one that carried wood and cargo in open wagons. In the dark, we jumped on board as soon as the train started to move. Days and nights passed by. It sounded as if the rail joints were singing: southward, southward, southward. Rome was going to be our second last stop.

CHAPTER 16

FINDING LOVE

After the end of the war, Rome became a gathering-place for people from many different countries. Refugees and allied soldiers, mostly Americans and British, dominated the street life. After the fall of Mussolini and the collapse of the fascism, the political situation was rather uncertain, but the influence of the British was great. Our orders were to carefully proceed in Rome, await directives and then continue toward the Italian southern coast. The group was dispersed so as not to arouse attention. We tried to disappear into the crowd, and it turned out to be quite easy to blend in among ordinary people on the lively streets of Rome. At the same time, Rome was a dangerous place for immigrants to Israel. Corruption and bribes are not new phenomenon in Italy. May people were unemployed after the war. Crime and prostitution occurred openly everywhere, outside the classical monuments. Squealing was also a profitable business. You had to watch out for the "friendly" Italians who wanted to earn a living.

The days in Rome became monotonous. I was eager to move to Israel before fall and the storms of Mediterranean turned the sea into an unreliable one and difficult to navigate. At last I received the news I had longed for, time for departure. I was going to a city in south Italy called Lecce, where I was supposed to join a kibbutz, a Jewish collective. There I had to wait my turn for a place on a boat. It was a terrific feeling to know I was so close to the destination.

I felt such a relief as soon as I sat down on the southbound train, which I hoped would be the last. Maybe that was the reason why I was so light-hearted. I rolled up the blanket into a pillow and put it behind my neck. I fell asleep and slept heavily and for a long time. I had no idea where I was or how long it had passed when I woke up. Suddenly I felt there was something wrong with my luggage. My bag! I still had my blanket, but my bag was gone. Trains in Italy, just like all trains in post-war-Europe were in poor condition. I was in a wagon with no windows. Someone must have stolen my bag through the wide-open window while I was asleep. The bag itself had no value to me. The only memory I had left from my family were the photos, my aunt in Budapest, gave me. Therefore, the bag was valuable to me. I panicked. The train slowed down at a station. A carbineer guarded that battered train station.

"I have been robbed," I shouted in all languages I could think of. "*Un ladro! Un ladro!* A thief!" Suddenly I remembered one of the few words in Italian I had intercepted.

"So what?" the carbineer told me. He spoke some kind of gibberish, which reminded me of German. Petty thefts were the trifles of everyday life. "Who cares? What had been stolen?" he asked. "Some photos?" He shook his head. Did I want to report such a small matter? Of course I would. But I realized how meaningless the whole thing was. I could never value my loss in money. And I would never be able to find the thief. I had lost something important, and I felt completely empty inside. Yet the journey must go on. I took my blanket and continued toward Lecce.

Despite the unpleasant bag incident, and all the horrible experiences I had endured, coming to Italy was like a dream. I eagerly embraced all the new impressions, the late summer days in Lecce offered me. Everything was new, exciting and stimulating to the imagination. With wide-open mind, I took in everything that surrounded me: fruits, flowers I had never seen before, warm, imaginative colors and flavors. The sun warmed my heart and gave my life back to me. And, of course, girls and women, who in my opinion were wonderfully beautiful, in a very special way managed to awaken the feelings of a lonely and quite lost young man.

After a while, the days in Lecce became monotonous too. I felt that I had no time to lose. The journey across Mediterranean could be a hazardous business. At this time, there were many legendary contraband vessels, with captains who took huge risks, in order to transport Jews across the British territory, outside the coast of Palestine. Many of the vessels that transported emigrants across the Mediterranean were old, leaky, small cargo ships that barely held together and obviously lacked any type of modern technologies, such as a navigation system or radar. The British had vessels with strong engines and radar of the latest model. Even though the odds of disembarking refugees on the Palestinian coast were small, the coast was long and therefore difficult to guard. Many vessels managed to get by passed the British surveillance vessels.

In Italy, everything could be bought with money. If you were willing to pay well of course. Vessels that previously belonged to the Italian Navy, transported those who could afford to pay.

One of these was going to take me across Mediterranean for a staggering amount of money. Luckily, I had the support of the big organization and they had promised me a place would be arranged.

"Night is the mother of the day," a Swedish poet has said. In the midst of despair, there is new hope and new joy. During my time in Lecce, against all odds, I began to feel stronger and regain a more positive outlook on life. For a long time, I had felt quite miserable. I had lost everything and everyone who mattered to me. I had no home. Ever since the liberation, most of my energy was consumed by keeping up the courage. Physically, I was in a terrible shape, lot worse than I dared to admit. As long as I had the journey to Israel as my main goal, I didn't sense anything of the illness that had affected my body. I guess we, as humans are more capable than we think, when we are in need. But every endeavor has its cost. Soon, I was about to learn that I had wasted my very last ounce of strength.

At the same time, something happened that truly felt like a miracle. At the kibbutz, I met Eva. She walked toward me, warm and intense, with beautiful dark eyes, pitch-black hair, and a funny scar on her chin. I fell in love with her, the moment I saw her for the very first time. Soon enough I found out she felt the same about me. This gave me a whole new perspective of the future. We enjoyed each other's company on a deep level, which somehow could compensate for the loss we both had experienced.

Her brother and older sister had leadership positions in the organization. They were both politically active and committed Zionists, since before the war. They convinced us that we had our future in the new land of Israel. If I had any doubts before, they were gone now. We waited for our departure and after a while we received news we would be on our way shortly. Suddenly I was taken ill. I was transported to the hospital two miles from Lecce, remotely located in between the mountains. The place was called Santa Maria de Leuca. At the hospital I was diagnosed with a severe bilateral tuberculosis. My x-ray results showed I had large holes in both lungs. I coughed terribly and spit blood. It had been an unusually warm summer. Scirocco, the wind that blows over Italy in summertime, brought in hot air from Sahara. The heat was abnormal. It probably was the triggering factor of my condition. The bleeding couldn't be stopped. The day of departure was approaching. Eva was inconsolable. "I cannot leave without you," she said.

"I will come soon after you," I replied, even though both of us knew it was a lie. The fact I had a deadly disease, which was also contagious, left me with no choice but to persuade her to go, although my heart was against it.

She left as planned on the boat that was supposed to take both of us across Mediterranean. I had survived all the rigors of the war, all the restless wandering from place to place. Now I had found peace and hope for the future in my relationship with Eva. I knew, I was dying but I was no longer afraid to die. I awaited the end with total indifference. *Come, death*, I thought. *You stupid death. You don't scare me anymore.*

I tried to get in touch with Eva several times after she left, but to no avail. Many years later, when I visited Israel, I managed to find her phone number. Eva lived in Jerusalem. Of course, I gave her a call. "Eva! Is that you?"

"Yes. Who is asking?" she said.

"Have a guess," I replied. Despite all my efforts to help her in the right direction, she could not understand who she was talking to. I was both disappointed and slightly confused by her reaction. How could she, the greatest love of my life, forget me so easily? When I told her who I was, there was complete silence on the other side. "Eva, are you there?"

"Yes! I cannot talk. We have to meet," she said in a low voice.

The next day I met Eva at her home in Jerusalem.

The reason why Eva couldn't believe at first was because shortly after her departure from Italy she was told I had passed away. The rumor had reached her via some mutual acquaintances, who had visited me at the first hospital where I laid dying. Since they were concerned for her and didn't want her to wait for me, they told her that I was dead. During our conversation that day, she showed me an envelope in which she had kept all our love letters. The papers had turned yellow. They were frayed on the edges, but still there, kept safely after all those years. So we found each other again, even though we had gone separate ways.

Back to Italy. One year had passed since the liberation and the end of the war. I was only twenty-two years old, but I had already experienced so much pain that I thought life had nothing more to offer. Nowadays it is obvious people who are in mentally poor shape often struggle with physical illness as well. The will to live itself could indeed be crucial in a fatal illness.

Strangely enough, you can always find help when you need it the most and expect it the least. There was a priest at the hospital, who visited the patients. He visited me daily and sat by my bedside. He didn't seem to care that I had another religion, which was considered to be hostile to his own. We became friends. He was just as surprised every day to see me alive. His thoughtfulness kept me in a good mood, even though I was dying.

It is said man plans, but God determines. Sometimes miracles do happen. In my case, it started with a letter. Someone from my group who had arrived in Palestine, after a few perilous days at sea, happened to make contact with my cousin. And told him that I was alive. My cousin had emigrated to Israel before the war. Apparently, my cousin had great news for me, so he wrote a letter and sent it to the kibbutz in Lecce. The boy who received the letter, understood that he had to deliver it to me at once. So he borrowed an old bicycle and left right away. The distance between the headquarter and the hospital was two miles. It may not seem as such a long distance, but there were no buses or trains, only a barely passable donkey trail that wriggled through rough terrain. He biked as much as he could, but he probably had to walk mostly on foot. Several hours later, he stood in front of me, breathless and sweaty. "A letter," he said. "Hope it is good news!" He helped me open the envelope and carefully I started to read the tightly written letter. One of my sisters was alive, and that was the most important thing in the letter. She had ended up in Sweden in a most unlikely way. The country was completely unknown to me. It was located outside all map books I had ever seen in school, and the name of the place where my sister lived didn't help at all. It is always hard to describe great emotions. The news of my sister being alive was absolutely the most powerful experience in my life, after the war and maybe even today. The letter gave me strength and I regained the will to live. Something happened that the doctors didn't want to acknowledge, at first. The bleeding ceased after a few days. My condition became remarkably much better, so the doctor took me in for a new x-ray examination. "*Ancora una volta*," (One more time) the nurse said. The examination was done again. None of the doctors at the hospital could believe what they saw. The x-ray results showed that great progress had occurred in a very short time. After being considered a hopeless case, I now received the best treatment the little hospital had to offer.

Miracles take time in real life. It would take more than four years of hospitalization until I was well enough to travel to Sweden and be reunited with my sister. When we finally met each other in calm and safe conditions, we were about to encounter an unexpected difficulty. It turned out to be almost impossible to talk about those horrid circumstances during World War II and everything that happened at the concentration camps. And we still are silent before one another. We both know we have suffered terribly. But still, more than sixty years later, the pain is so great that makes it hard to talk about the people we lost and probably what has reshaped us as human beings. It is also one reason why I decided to tell my story. I know one thing for sure: words set you free.

CHAPTER 17

FROM THE END TO A NEW BEGINNING

Now, after reading this book, you have more knowledge about the events that occurred during the Second World War and also about the evil mechanisms at work during the war. Knowledge about how we can cooperate and contribute in order to build a better life for everyone. Knowledge about what we can learn from history, for it is only through the lessons of history that we stand a chance to prevent the history from repeating itself.

And think about it: You now have a better understanding of the answer I gave to a student who asked me this question: "How has the war changed you?"

"I value life more, and I think of others. But basically, I am the same person as I was before the war because I was brought up in a warm, loving family, and that gave me a good foundation to stand on."

I would like to finish my book with a challenge for you: None of us are powerful enough to help the entire world. But each and every one of us can make a small effort to help someone in our immediate vicinity, as we should always start there. How else can we expect people far away from us to stop fighting and killing each other unless we are able to create mutual understanding by helping someone close to us in need?

www.ingramcontent.com/pod-product-compliance
Lightning Source LLC
Chambersburg PA
CBHW020444090526
44586CB00045B/853